"A feminist anthem for the Palestinian revolution, *Palestine and Feminist Liberation* draws us into the heart of the matter: decolonial feminist and queer resistance is not only vital to Palestinian freedom, Palestinian liberation is indispensable to the shared future, praxis, and transformative potential of decolonial feminism itself."

Dr. Sarah Ihmoud, assistant professor, Department of Anthropology, College of the Holy Cross; founding member, Palestinian Feminist Collective

"In the struggle against genocide, dehumanization, collective erasure, and land theft, Palestinian feminists have always played a key role in the resistance against settler colonialism. *Palestine and Feminist Liberation* is a must-read for anyone fighting for justice from Turtle Island to Palestine."

Katsi'tsakwas Ellen Gabriel, author of *When the Pine Needles Fall: Indigenous Acts of Resistance*

"Nada Elia's essays on Palestine and feminism come at the exact right moment. Framed by an incisive introduction by the author and a compelling closing interview, Elia lays out with clarity and concision how Palestinian liberation is part and parcel of a feminist and queer struggle, and delivers a searing critique of how the feminism of the Global North missed the structural underpinnings of Palestinian oppression for far too long."

Jen Marlowe, writer, filmmaker, activist, and founder of Donkeysaddle Projects

"In *Palestine and Feminist Liberation*, Elia reminds us that Palestine is a feminist issue. She insists that we look to feminists in Palestine and to diaspora Palestinian feminists on Turtle Island and throughout the world so we may begin or strengthen our commitments to their liberation, as well as our commitments to collective empowerment and liberation for oppressed people everywhere."

Heidi R. Lewis, professor, Feminist and Gender Studies, Colorado College

Palestine and Feminist Liberation

Nada Elia

Between the Lines
Toronto

Palestine and Feminist Liberation
© 2025 Nada Elia

First published in French by les Éditions du remue-ménage as Palestine: Un féminisme de libération © Nada Elia et les Éditions du remue-ménage, 2024. "Decolonial Feminism and Palestine: An Interview with Nada Elia" English translation © 2025 Sarah Moses.

This edition published in 2025 by
Between the Lines
401 Richmond Street West, Studio 281
Toronto, Ontario · M5V 3A8 · Canada
1-800-718-7201 · www.btlbooks.com

Library and Archives Canada Cataloguing in Publication
Title: Palestine and feminist liberation / Nada Elia.
Names: Elia, Nada, author
Series: Provocations (Toronto, Ont.)
Description: Series statement: Provocations | Includes bibliographical references. | Some chapters originally published in French, translated into English for this work. Some chapters originally published in English, and were translated into French in another work.
Identifiers: Canadiana (print) 20250237253 | Canadiana (ebook) 20250242761 | ISBN 9781771136891 (softcover) | ISBN 9781771136907 (EPUB)
Subjects: LCSH: Women, Palestinian Arab—Social conditions. | LCSH: Women, Palestinian Arab—Political activity. | LCSH: Feminism—Palestine. | LCSH: Anti-imperialist movements—Palestine.
Classification: LCC HQ1728.5 .E4513 2025 | DDC 305.48/89274—dc23

Cover and text design by DEEVE
Frontispiece: Funeral for a ten-year-old boy from Jalazone refugee camp, north of Ramallah, killed by Isreali Occupation Forces soldiers in 1990.
Photo: Mahfouz Abu Turk.

Printed in Canada

We acknowledge for their financial support of our publishing activities: the Government of Canada; the Canada Council for the Arts; and the Government of Ontario through the Ontario Arts Council, the Ontario Book Publishers Tax Credit program, and Ontario Creates.

 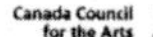     

Contents

Global Intifada

Since October 7, 2023, I have been waking up multiple times every night, checking my phone for updates from Gaza. As the weeks turn into months, and now years, new questions and fears arise. With the Israeli-manufactured famine gripping the entire population of the Gaza Strip, how many hundreds of starving Palestinians will be executed at aid distribution centres, how many more thousands of Palestinians will be massacred, before Israel's genocide of the Palestinian people is finally put to an end? How long would it take to rebuild a region where over 90 percent of all buildings, homes, places of worship, libraries, museums, office buildings, medical centres and hospitals, and all the schools and universities, have been destroyed? What about Gaza's children, over 40 percent of whom have lost at least one parent since October 7, 2023? What about the hundreds who are losing an arm or a leg, or more, every single day since that fateful date? What about those who are losing their vision, their hearing, whose health will be impacted for the rest of their lives because of the famine Israel is imposing on their developing bodies?

How will we overcome the pain, the sadness, the trauma?

How much longer can this genocide continue?

Palestinians and our allies know that our genocide did not begin on October 7, 2023, in the wrathful aftermath of Hamas's attack on southern Israel. This is why we insist on speaking of an *accelerated* genocide, an *intensified* genocide, as we explain the historical context of the October 7 attack. Israel has been dispossessing and murdering Palestinians since its very inception in 1948, and even prior to that, when Zionist militias terrorized and massacred civilians from Balad el-Sheikh to Saasaa to Deir Yassin, before Israel even became a country. Zionist militias, and later Israeli fighters, engaged in a violent process of ethnic cleansing, expelling hundreds of thousands of Palestinians from their homes not just after October 7, 2023, but at the very onset of the Nakba, in 1948. As these fighters claimed more and more of our land, Palestinian families were separated, thousands were murdered, women were raped, and children orphaned. Hundreds of thousands of Palestinians who were displaced in 1948 were never allowed to return to their towns and villages, just as today, Israeli soldiers are preventing Palestinians displaced within Gaza itself from returning to their homes. This is why we also speak of "the onset of the Nakba," which is ongoing and has never relented, even though we commemorate it on a specific day, May 15, of every year.

The Gaza Strip, where today we are witnessing this accelerated genocide, is a tiny segment of historic Palestine, a mere 1.5 percent of our homeland. It is one of the most densely populated areas of the world, with 2.3 million Palestinians, 80 percent of whom are refugees from other parts of historic Palestine. Many have been displaced multiple times; most have lived through multiple wars. When they attacked the partygoers at the Nova rave and the settlers in two kibbutzim in southern Israel, the Hamas militants were breaching a sixteen-year-old illegal blockade that had already reduced life for Palestinians in the Gaza Strip to a daily struggle for mere survival. As early as 2006, Dov Weissglas, an adviser to Ehud Olmert, Israel's prime minister at the time, summed up his country's policy towards the illegally occupied strip by explaining: "The idea is to put the Palestinians on a diet, but not to make them die of hunger." That was before the chokehold of the siege was imposed, in 2007. Since then, Israel has launched four military assaults on Gaza: in 2008, 2012, 2014, and 2021. Each of these attacks exacerbated Gaza's already dire situation. What we are witnessing today, then, is a continuation of Israel's practices rather than a divergence from these.

Yet even as we insist that this is an accelerated but not novel genocide, we are also deeply aware that we are living a historical moment, one of global transformation. Of course, Palestinians have always known that Israel is a violent, racist, settler-colonial state founded on genocide and maintained through the persistent violation of international law and the human rights of the Palestinian people. But now, this is becoming common knowledge among many who were "Zionist by default" until recently; those who had unquestioningly absorbed the Zionist narrative, which presents Israel, rather than the Palestinians, as the victim in this historic injustice. But it is becoming harder every day, with every new Israeli atrocity, for anyone but the most deranged Zionist to conceive of Israel's savagery as defence.

And as people on Turtle Island are connecting the dots between their own oppression and that of the Palestinian people, they are awaking from their slumber. Speaking as a diaspora Palestinian on Turtle Island, I am seeing the growing recognition of the interconnectedness of our struggles when Americans grasp that their government donates billions of their tax dollars to Israel, which could be used to improve the dilapidated public schools across this country, offer US citizens health insurance and public housing for those in need, or cancel crushing student debts. We know that the hypermilitarized police in US cities have been trained by Israeli police, Israeli occupation soldiers, and the Shin Bet. We recognize that the "knee-on-neck" stranglehold used against George Floyd is the same as that used by Israeli soldiers against Palestinian children. We understand that the struggles of the wretched of the earth everywhere are interconnected, that the reason children are hungry and sick people are dying of preventable diseases in the world's richest country while the mentally ill are incarcerated rather than treated in medical institutions is because the US government is more interested in the prison industrial complex, and the military-industrial complex, than in sustaining life, both abroad and within its borders.

There is a global intifada underway, with millions of us taking to the streets in towns and cities around the world to protest these oppressive systems, the purveyors of death, disease, and misery. Our numbers are growing daily.

At this pivotal moment, then, as the protests against state-sanctioned violence from Seattle to Palestine keep swelling, we must already be thinking about the future. Abolishing an oppressive system without having sufficiently prepared the scaffolding for the new liberated society to thrive is a recipe for failure, as we can see in many postcolonial, postrevolutionary countries around the world. It is therefore important for us to look globally and to learn from the past, from other communities that have endured racism, apartheid, colonialism, occupation. We cannot afford more of the same, more politics as usual, we must not agree to the concessions demanded of the oppressed and dispossessed, we cannot conduct more "negotiation" processes, more peace talks, and launch more false starts that lead nowhere.

Fortunately, we do not need to start from scratch; there are models from which we can draw inspiration, which have sustained us so far. Palestine will be liberated by its youth, who are determined to see freedom, justice, and Indigenous sovereignty within their own lifetime and are disrupting business as usual until they achieve this. They are the ones who rise against their oppressor again and again, celebrating rather than squashing the impulse to live freely, in dignity. Palestine will be liberated by its proud peasants, the resilient men, women, and children whose insistence that they would rather die than leave their homeland reminds the world that we as a people remain, steadfast, not because we want to own the land but because we belong to it. It will be liberated by its feminist organizers, who understand that there can be no free homeland without free women and queers.

These marginalized communities have never been represented in the halls of power, and from internal teach-ins to mutual aid networks, they have had to create alternative systems for collective empowerment. They are our models, and now is the time to uplift the life-sustaining systems they have envisioned and crafted. We cannot look yet again at the politicians, the mediators, the "negotiators" who have failed to give us justice, who have failed to end seventy-seven years of displacement, fifty-eight years of a brutal military occupation, and eighteen years of stranglehold on a besieged, intentionally de-developed sliver of land, the repeatedly battered last refuge for generations of refugees.

We need to uplift the alternative models of life giving and life sustaining, the transformational models of the downtrodden. We owe it to our heroes, our heroines. We owe it to our martyrs. We owe it to our children. Not repeating the mistakes of the past is a duty, but it's also an act of love towards the new generation of Palestinians. I hope this modest book will provide a glimpse into the role Palestinian women have historically played in our collective liberation.

Nada Elia
Writing from the ancestral land
of the Coast Salish people
June 2025

ONE

Multiple Jeopardy
Gender and Liberation in Palestine

> We have more strength than any man. The strength that I showed the first day of the protests, I dare you to find it in anyone else.
>
> —Razan Najjar (2014)

Palestinian women and queers in the homeland are often asked by concerned Westerners how we negotiate the challenges of living full, rewarding lives in a conservative society. Those of us in the Western diaspora are asked if we are not better off, really, living in "modern" societies, where we can wear whatever we want, go wherever we want. These questions are misguided. Instead, Palestinians should be asked how we persist, how we continue to live, love, and care, in a society that is living under a brutal system of apartheid intent on erasing our very existence and history. We should be asked how we persist under the rule of law of an ethno-supremacist country that views each and every one of us as a "demographic threat" simply for being who we are. We should be asked how our youth retain the impulse to be free when trigger-happy Israeli soldiers and snipers are

Reprinted with permission from "Multiple Jeopardy: Gender and Liberation in Palestine" in *Palestine: A Socialist Introduction*, Sumaya Awad and brian bean, eds. (Haymarket, 2020), 210–224.

ordered to kill unarmed children demanding their human rights. We should be asked how we continue to build community, nurture each other, and denounce settler colonialism in the same breath as we reject patriarchy. And anyone who is concerned that those of us in the diaspora are better off than in Palestine should stop and think about who the greater oppressor of the Palestinian people, including women and queers, is: Israel, which denies every Palestinian their basic rights, or Palestinian society, with its at times stifling "traditional values," which are often little more than an attempt to hold on to one's culture, threatened with erasure.[1] And they should consider that, for the millions of us longing for the homeland, our diaspora is not a choice but a reality imposed upon the Palestinian people by Israel.

I begin, reluctantly, with a brief discussion of the Western discourse on Palestine because I believe it is of critical importance to our circumstances, as the question of Palestine is a global one, with close to 80 percent of the entire Palestinian people forcibly displaced from their ancestral towns and villages, while Israel, which dispossessed us, receives financial support and political immunity from Western powers.[2] Indeed, the recognition of the West's critical role in ending the oppression of the Palestinian people is implicit in the fact that the liberation strategy agreed upon by a broad coalition of Palestinian civil society organizations, namely the Boycott, Divestment, and Sanctions (BDS) movement, hinges on global solidarity by individuals living in those countries that can impact Israel—and these happen to be mostly in the West. Nevertheless, as far as the mainstream discourse in the West is concerned, Palestinian women and queers either do not exist or are oppressed by "Islamic fundamentalism," with little recognition of Israel's violence, much of which is gendered.

The long-standing Western refusal to address Palestinian women's struggles was made clear in 1985, when a patronizing Betty Friedan, an icon of Western feminism, with its "the personal is political" rallying call, attempted to censor the prominent Egyptian feminist Nawal El Saadawi at the United Nations International Conference on Women in Nairobi, Kenya. "Please do not bring up Palestine in your speech," Friedan told El Saadawi. And in a stunning demonstration of bad faith and intellectual laziness, both stemming from unfettered racism, Friedan "explained" to the fiery Arab feminist that "this is a women's conference, not a political conference."[3]

Friedan obviously had no clue who she was dealing with. As El Saadawi later wrote, in a clear articulation of Palestinian women's circumstances:

> Of course in my speech, I did not heed what she [Friedan] had said to me since I believe that women's issues cannot be dealt with in isolation from politics. The emancipation of women in the Arab region is closely linked to the regimes under which we live, regimes which are supported by the USA in most cases, and the struggle between Israel and Palestine has an important impact on the political situation. Besides, how can we speak of liberation for Palestinian women without speaking of their right to have a land

on which to live? How can we speak about Arab women's rights in Palestine and Israel without opposing the racial discrimination exercised against them by the Israeli regime?[4]

White/Western feminism's attempt at erasing the political context of Palestinian women's oppression was evident yet again around the 2017 Women's March on Washington, when liberal feminists objected to the leadership of Palestinian American organizer Linda Sarsour, and the newly-minted "Zionesses" complained of "antisemitism" because Palestinian women's circumstances were on the platform as part of a broader discussion of US president Donald Trump's Muslim ban and the overall Islamophobia he pandered to. Interestingly, the "Zioness Movement" itself sprouted on the US activist scene with the explicit intention to counter feminists who were successfully denouncing Zionism. It chose the slogan "Unabashedly progressive, unapologetically Zionist" in direct response to the growing if belated understanding among many Western feminists that Zionism is racism and has no place in progressive movements.[5] This understanding had become obvious, for example, when the largest academic women's organization, the National Women's Studies Association, voted in favour of BDS at its November 2015 annual convention. Meanwhile, in street protests and at LGBTQ meetings, anti-Zionist activists in cities from Seattle, Washington, to Berlin, Germany, were also rallying in support of Palestinian rights, disrupting "pinkwashing" events, and leading major national marches.

Pinkwashing is Israel's smoke-and-mirrors attempt to distract from its egregious human rights record by foregrounding its own supposed gender liberalism while directing an accusing finger at Palestinian society. Anti-pinkwashing activists have successfully disrupted such propaganda by pointing out that Israeli society overall is quite conservative; Israel is only "gay-friendly" when it serves its political purposes and only when individual gay people are Israelis or the much-coveted Western tourists.[6] Simply put, Israel does not make exceptions for queer Palestinian refugees when it comes to the denial of their right of return; an Israeli soldier does not inquire about a Palestinian individual's sexuality as they go through a checkpoint, letting queers through while detaining straight Palestinians; and house demolition crews do not spare the homes of gay Palestinians.[7]

It is in this context of the complete erasure of Palestinian women (and more generally, but not as consistently, Arab and Muslim women as well) that one must understand the statement made by former US secretary of state Madeleine Albright as she rallied for Hillary Clinton—a solid booster of the apartheid state—in the 2016 presidential campaign: "There is a special place in hell for women who do not help each other."[8] Albright later apologized for that comment, just as she had earlier apologized for answering a question about the deaths of half a million Iraqi children as a result of US sanctions with, "We think the price is worth it."[9]

Meanwhile, in Palestine itself, women and queers have all along been actively resisting their own "special place in hell," battered by Western imperialism and

Israel's unrelenting genocidal intent on the one hand and Palestinian culture's lingering patriarchal values on the other. In the masculinist, patriarchal dominant discourse, "struggle," especially "national struggle," is generally understood as armed resistance. Yet armed resistance is only one of many ways Palestinians have fought their oppression, and certainly not the most effective, as it has never achieved any lasting victories. Another, more comprehensive understanding of "resistance" would take into consideration all the ways we persevere against the odds—that is, our *sumoud* (steadfastness) when Zionists are intent on erasing our very existence. As the popular Palestinian saying goes, "Our mere existence is resistance."

Specifically, Palestinian women's resistance is as old as the national struggle itself, predating the 1948 Nakba, and has taken many forms, from the unarmed storming of British Mandate barracks, the sheltering of orphans, and the behind-the-scenes political organizing throughout the First Intifada to community building in the diaspora, fostering safe spaces for queers, providing Palestinian children access to playgrounds, and insisting on Palestinian rights to the US Congress. It is often observed that history is written by the victors. What is not sufficiently denounced, except in feminist narratives, is that history is also primarily a record of men's fighting, with rarely any mention of women's contributions unless these happen to have taken place in traditionally masculine fields. (Leila Khaled, for example, who hijacked planes, is much better known than Hind al-Husseini, discussed below, who sheltered orphans.) Nevertheless, knowing and understanding a society requires that we look to its alternative history, which only seldom makes it into textbooks. And while no list of Palestinian women's accomplishments in this alternative history can possibly be exhaustive, it is helpful to give a brief sampling of such achievements so as to best illustrate the multiple ways we, as Palestinian women, are navigating the murky waters.

Beginning almost a century ago, when Palestine was still under British Mandate, with a very strict martial law imposed on the Palestinian people, Palestinian women were already organizing against colonialism. In fact, throughout the 1920s, women were marching side by side with men in protests against Britain's plan to give part of their homeland to European Jewish settlers—a plan first made public in the Balfour Declaration of 1917, which Britain promptly set into action by facilitating the influx of Jewish immigrants, even as it forcefully repressed Palestinian opposition to their dispossession.[10] The harshness of the British Mandate may pale in comparison to the horrors of Zionism, with its insatiable expansionist ambitions, yet its impact should not be overlooked as we survey Palestinian women's contributions to their society's resistance to imperialism and settler colonialism. For example, members of the Arab Women's Union in Jerusalem, established in 1929, were active participants in political protests; they provided shelter and medical aid to fighters and played a pioneering role in raising social awareness about the importance of women's liberation to the overall well-being of their society. The General Union of Palestinian Women, an umbrella organization for various Palestinian women's groups, founded in 1965, remains active today in both the social and political spheres and links gender equality with national liberation. The Palestinian Women's Work Committees, formed in the late 1970s, focused on the mass recruitment of women; as a result, today many women's organizations have memberships in the thousands, addressing the many challenges facing Palestinian women, from education to employment to national liberation.[11]

One of the early examples of Palestinian women's resistance to colonialism happened in the late 1930s,[12] when the British stormed the militant village of Baqa al-Gharbiya, near Haifa, burning down its houses and taking away all its men to a nearby camp—sadly, a common occurrence as the British were quashing Palestinian resistance to their imperial plans. That same night, the village women, "armed" only with rocks, descended upon the barracks and successfully secured the release of the men. Throughout the mandate, women continued to contribute directly to the resistance by selling their jewellery in order to purchase guns for fighters, even though there was a very strict British ban against Palestinians having any weapons, with hefty penalties for possession. Women also formed social clubs that acted as and evolved into fronts for political organizing. These groups maintained the social network essential for any functional society whose men had to go into hiding or were exiled for their participation in the revolt against the imperial plan to dispossess them.

The British Mandate gave way to Jewish Zionism's

stranglehold on Palestine, and any serious overview of Palestinian women's contribution to the survival and well-being of our society must pay tribute to Jerusalemite Hind al-Husseini, who used her personal privilege to found Dar al-Tifl al-Arabi, an orphanage she established in 1948 and that continues to offer Palestinian children shelter, education, food, and fun to this day. In April 1948, after Zionist militia raided the village of Deir Yassin, killing, decapitating, and raping a majority of the adults in one of the many horrific massacres predating the bloody birth of Israel, the Jewish terrorists rounded up fifty-five orphaned children, most of whom were under nine years old, and paraded them in Palestine's capital city to be stoned and spat on, before abandoning them there, homeless, terrified, cold, and hungry.[13] When Hind al-Husseini, a member of the prominent Jerusalemite family, saw the children, she took them all under her aegis, first housing them in two rooms in a nearby market, where she visited with them daily, comforting them and feeding them, then moving them to a convent before moving them again one last time to her own family home, a mansion built by her grandfather in the Sheikh Jarrah area of Jerusalem. Al-Husseini went on to purchase two additional buildings and continued to take care of these children, and thousands more over the years, until she passed away in 1994. Her legacy lives on to this day, as Dar al-Tifl, or "the children's home," as it is better known, now has the capacity to board three hundred children, accepting only girls, either orphaned or from impoverished families, and offering them shelter, education, food, sports, arts, and extracurricular activities. Its goals, according to its website, are:

> Taking care of female Palestinian orphan and needy children, providing them with a good decent life. Establishing schools to teach and educate girls in addition to training them to be self-independent. Sponsoring extracurricular activities, establishing literary, scientific, and art clubs with sport activities towards developing their talents. Preserving the Arab and the Palestinian heritage and culture.

In addition to Dar al-Tifl, Hind al-Husseini also established a school for social work and a women's college, which were later transferred to Al-Quds University, as well as a museum and a cultural centre.

Like many women of her generation, al-Husseini was also very active in a number of social organizations that evolved into more openly political[14] work as Palestine was catapulted into survival mode after the Nakba—the catastrophe that befell Palestinians with the creation of Israel. These organizations remained active as Israel tightened its grip on Palestinian lives and land. This uninterrupted activism by women who had an experiential understanding that no nation can be "free" until all its members, men and women, are free and equal, is beautifully depicted in Julia Bacha's documentary *Naila and the Uprising*. Bacha had not intentionally set out to make a feminist film, focused on women and gender dynamics, when she first decided to make a documentary about the First Intifada. Instead, she was primarily concerned with recording an important moment in Palestinian history that is frequently misrepresented. Her vision evolved as she conducted field research and interviewed participants in the grassroots movement. As Bacha writes in her director's notes, what she discovered was that women were instrumental in coordinating the popular social upheaval and often exploited Israeli society's own patriarchal assumptions to coordinate the uprising. Indeed, as one of the women in the documentary explains, women were less likely to be arrested after curfew and less likely to be searched, so they could transport leaflets or cloth with which to stitch together Palestinian flags.[15] As the film's website explains, "While most images of the First Intifada paint an incomplete picture of stone-throwing young men front and center, this film tells the story that history overlooked—of an unbending, nonviolent women's movement at the head of Palestine's struggle for freedom."[16] The women in this uprising, still referred to as "the intifada of the stones," mobilized hundreds of thousands of civilians, ran mobile health clinics, organized underground schools when Israel forcefully shut down Palestinian schools, and launched Indigenous self-sustainability initiatives so as to allow Palestinians to boycott Israeli products.

Bacha writes:

The First Intifada was not only a vibrant, strategic and sustained nonviolent civil resistance movement; for months, it was also led by a network of Palestinian women who were fighting a dual struggle for national liberation and gender equality. We knew we wanted to bring this story to light by producing a documentary that could provide insight and wisdom from the veteran women activists of the First Intifada to today's rising leader . . . From the First Intifada to the present moment, it's clear: women's leadership in civil society organizing is vital. But too often, their work is sidelined or ignored . . . Women have consistently been a part of influential social movements coming out of the Middle East, but time and again, the cameras focus on armed men, leaving us with a narrative that not only erases women but also misrepresents the struggles themselves, as well as the demands behind those struggles.[17]

Just as the French colonizers had completely misunderstood Algerian women's contribution to the Algerian revolution, assuming that those in "modern" (Western) dress could not possibly be anti-French, so too with the Israelis, who did not suspect that some of the "well-dressed" Palestinian women were also radical activists and organizers. Eventually, as more Palestinian men were arrested and/or deported, women took the helm of most social organizations, from prisoners' committees to community sustainability. These Palestinian women, the backbone of the First Intifada, had an incisive analysis of social norms and were intentional about resisting and challenging both Israel's violations of their human rights and their own society's restrictive gender roles. Today, along with the denunciation of the disastrous outcome of the Oslo Accords, which put an end to the First Intifada, there is a growing realization that the accords also dealt a serious blow to women's emancipation and the social gains they had achieved as they led the grassroots social uprising. Bacha comments on that unfortunate development in the director's notes about *Naila and the Uprising*: "The film is also a cautionary tale for what happens when women are stripped of their leadership roles and excluded from ongoing struggles."[18]

Western feminists have been and remain quick to denounce the oppression of Arab women as a result of Islamic fundamentalism but not as a result of Israeli occupation, and they seem oblivious to the fact that occupation and militarism have gendered manifestations that aggravate women's circumstances in Palestine, as they would anywhere else. This is all the more surprising when these feminist scholars are eager to analyze the feminization of poverty in other war-ravaged countries, the disenfranchisement of women as military institutions hold sway over a society, the violence of sex work and sexual slavery in war zones, and the overall increase in sexual violence in communities that have experienced armed conflict. When it comes to Israel, however, many Western feminists' critical analysis collapses into a reductionist binary that views Israel as "Western," "modern," "civilized" and Palestinians as "backwards" and thus fails to grasp the gendered aspects of Israel's oppression of the Palestinian people. The myopic lens looks only at the microenvironment, namely Arab society, and completely overlooks the macroenvironment, namely Israel's occupation. Yet, as many Palestinian feminists have documented over the past decades, Israel's violence is gendered, impacting women in multiple ways, from the denial of health and reproductive rights to sexual torture in prison. And, in what can only be viewed as an extreme stretch of the definition of "gay-friendly," Israel has also pressured queers in Gaza and the West Bank into collaborating with the occupiers by threatening to out them to their conservative families unless they spy on members of their own communities. And, of course, as psychological and physical torture are rampant in Israeli jails, so is sexual violence, including rape.

The documentary *Women in Struggle*, by Buthina Canaan Khoury, follows four Palestinian women political prisoners after their release from Israeli jail as they narrate their experience in Israeli detention. One, Rasmea Odeh, was subjected to extreme torture and raped with a broomstick when her father, who was brought into the room with her and ordered to rape her, refused to do so. Forced to confess, Odeh was sentenced to life in prison for allegedly detonating a bomb in a café that resulted in the death of two Israeli students. Following her release after ten years, as part of a larger prisoners' exchange, she emigrated to the US in 1995, obtained US citizenship in 2004, and became a cherished leader of the Arab American community in Chicago.

Catapulted into prominence by her struggle against a corrupt justice system that eventually stripped her of her citizenship and deported her on the basis of a confession made under torture, Odeh has become a symbol for millions of women who identify with aspects of her multifaceted experience.

Odeh represents today's organic, grassroots leader. Her credentials come from decades of community work, empowering immigrant women and building community. A criminalized, marginalized Palestinian immigrant survivor of settler colonialism, militarism, imprisonment, and physical, sexual, and psychological torture, she exposed Israel as a racist occupier and colonizer to communities of immigrants, feminists, and Black and brown people she had organized alongside for decades.

Meanwhile, back in Palestine, one group that has done important work in addressing the multiple jeopardy of Palestinian women and queers generally, under the capable leadership of Haneen Maikey, is AlQaws for Gender Diversity and Sexual Diversity in Palestinian Society (*AlQaws* is Arabic for "rainbow"). AlQaws's vision is grounded in the understanding that there is no separating the personal from the political—the same understanding expressed by Nawal El Saadawi at the 1985 International Conference on Women—as articulated in its statement on its political vision:

> Our work strategies and programs emerge directly from our field experience and careful analysis of the concrete local reality that shapes current social and cultural attitudes around sexual and gender diversity. For Palestinian society, all grassroots work is affected by Israeli colonialism and occupation. And, alQaws has been demonstrating for over a decade that all political work intersects with issues that are sometimes dismissed as too personal, apolitical, or irrelevant to anti-occupation and de-colonial organizing, such as homosexuality and queer identity, non-normative gender, and so on. In all of our work,

we aim to expand our impact on our society through an ever-increasing circle of partners and supporters who adopt our vision, while standing firm in our beliefs and values. Our commitment to supporting and strengthening Palestinian queer/LGBT communities cannot be separated from our vision for a self-determined Palestinian society free from all forms of oppression.[19]

The multiple forms of oppression became clear in the summer of 2019, when in response to AlQaws announcing that it would be running a number of workshops for queer youth in the West Bank, the group came under attack by none other than Palestinian Authority president Mahmoud Abbas, who would not be in (symbolic) power himself were it not for the US and Israel.[20]

Earlier that summer, a young Palestinian had been severely stabbed in Tel Aviv by his own brother over suspicions about his sexuality. And shortly thereafter, the entire world heard the screams of the young Israa Ghrayyeb as she was beaten to death by her own family members, murdered for having gone to a café with her fiancé, not yet husband.[21]

These horrific incidents were loudly denounced by Palestinians within Palestine itself, who took to the streets in protests carrying signs proclaiming that "Patriarchy Kills" and "there is no honour in honour crimes." Hundreds also joined protests specifically against homophobia, with signs highlighting that Palestinian queers should not have to take refuge in their occupier's gay-friendly Tel Aviv to avoid their own society's homophobia. Indeed, the popular outrage at the stabbing of the gay teenager and the murder of Israa Ghrayyeb are indicative of the progress made within Palestinian society. The protests and the nascent Tal'at movement[22] are indicative of a widespread understanding that patriarchy is oppressive, even murderous, rather than "part of our traditions" and that it must be overthrown if Palestinian society is to be a healthy, resilient one. Simply, we would not be where we are now—survivors, leaders, organizers—were it not for our Palestinians mothers, grandmothers, and great-grandmothers, who have sustained Palestinian society for the better part of a century against tremendous odds from both within and without.

The memory of Razan Najjar is a reminder of this. On June 1, 2018, Razan was shot by an Israeli sniper while she tended to wounded protestors participating in the Great March of Return in Gaza. Razan was a paramedic, yet Israeli snipers targeted her despite her visible white coat. Weeks before she was murdered, she explained to a *New York Times* journalist what made her go out day after day, knowing snipers were shooting indiscriminately: "In our society women are often judged . . . But society has to accept us. If they don't want to accept us by choice, they will be forced to accept us because we have more strength than any man."

Today, Palestinian women and queers cross geographic, social, and gender borders as they proudly stand front and centre in progressive causes everywhere, just as Palestine itself is finally understood as a progressive, decolonial, Indigenous, feminist, and queer issue. And while it is only right that this understanding of the multiple jeopardy facing Palestinian women and queers comes from within these communities themselves, in the homeland as well as the diaspora, it is time for allies globally to also grasp that our circumstances can only be addressed through an anticolonial approach, free of imperialist feminism and Islamophobia.

Justice Is Indivisible

Palestine as a Feminist Issue

Allow me to return to Wafa Idris and where, at this historical juncture, do radical women of color, with our focus on intersections of race, class, gender, sexism, homophobia, colonialism, and imperialism, locate her? Will we explore the impact of colonization on Wafa's family? Palestinian families? Palestinian communities? . . . Will we take interest in Palestinian feminists' analysis of women's resistance? Where do we locate her in the context of feminist heroine metaphors that highlight women's transformations from passivity to agency? And how might feminist theorizations of the body grapple with a woman who deploys the body as weapon against an unstoppable military machine?

—Nadine Naber (2006)

We are still faced with the challenge of understanding the complex ways race, class, gender, sexuality, nation and ability are intertwined—but also how we move beyond these categories to understand the interrelationships of ideas and processes that seem to be

Reprinted from "Justice Is Indivisible: Palestine as a Feminist Issue," in *Decolonization: Indigeneity, Education & Society* 6, no. 1, 2017: 45-63.

separate and unrelated. Insisting on the connections between struggles and racism in the United States and struggles against the Israeli repression of Palestinians, in this sense, is a feminist process.

—Angela Davis (2016)

When the National Women's Studies Association (NWSA) voted by a landslide majority to endorse BDS at its annual convention in November 2015, Palestinian scholar-activist Rabab Abdulhadi spoke of a "browning of the organization," a demographic change within the largest Global North mainstream academic association dedicated to scholarship on gender.[1] That demographic change, Abdulhadi suggests, is behind the vote that not only acknowledges the oppression of the Palestinian people but also approves of and endorses a strategy they have proposed to end this oppression. BDS is the Palestinian call for global solidarity in the form of boycott of, divestment from, and sanctions on Israel until it abides by international law and ends its violations of the human rights of the Palestinian people. The call for BDS was issued in July 2005 and, ten years later, what was once a soft whisper limited to the margins of various progressive groups had become a chorus of voices clamouring for an end to Israel's egregious treatment of the Indigenous people whose land it is occupying. This discursive change, due in large part to the debates occasioned by BDS resolutions, represents a shattering of the Zionist mythology of Israeli "democracy" and frailty— its supposed vulnerability to a hostile and aggressive regional environment. And with the growing awareness among various communities that Israel is not an embattled democracy but a violently racist settler-colonial state comes a widespread desire to hold it accountable for its crimes. Indeed, arguably the most significant success of the BDS campaign so far has been the open discussion of Israeli violations of international law and of the human rights of the Palestinian people, a discussion that necessarily precedes every boycott and divestment vote by a city council, a co-op, a church, or a professional association. These discussions, debates, and open forums have torn asunder the Zionist narrative, which could only be maintained through silencing; the censorship of counter-histories.

The NWSA vote came on the heels of similar votes (preceded by lengthy discussions) by the Asian American Studies Association, the Native American and Indigenous Studies Association, and the American Studies Association, to name a few of the national professional academic associations. Other such groups have since also passed resolutions in favour of BDS, and many, such as the Modern Language Association, are in some stage of organizing for a resolution.

Yet while the NWSA membership has indeed changed since the group was established in 1977, one cannot assume that "brown feminism" is a monolith, nor that it has always been on board with anticolonial struggles, at least not as far as Palestine is involved. Nadine Naber's plea for consistency, cited in the epigraph to this essay, is proof that the plight of Palestinians has often been dismissed even in radical feminist circles. Yes, there are some long-standing alliances between

Palestinian and other communities-of-colour radicals. The San Francisco–based Women of Color Resource Center, for example, has historically been consistent in its denunciation of colonialism and racism and, under the able leadership of executive director Linda Burnham, identified Zionism as a form of racism as early as 2000. INCITE! Women of Color Against Violence issued its "Palestine Points of Unity" shortly after it was formed, albeit after much internal debate, proving that alliances are forged, earned, not spontaneous.

However, there are few Palestinian feminists who have not experienced some degree of suspicion, misunderstanding, or outright hostility within communities of colour, even feminist communities of colour. And the further we reach into (albeit-recent) history, the more that is the case. For, while it was obvious to some of the more radical Global North activists that our struggle was no different than the struggles of any colonized people, our yearning for liberation was all too often misread by many as anti-semitism rather than as an organic impulse to cherish freedom, dignity, and self-determination.[2] As Angela Davis put it: "The important issues in the Palestinian struggle for freedom and self-determination are minimized and rendered invisible by those who try to equate Palestinian resistance to Israeli apartheid with terrorism."[3] This is less frequent today, but certainly not a thing of the past, nor a perspective that prevails only among white feminists. In fact, these "important issues" are rendered invisible to most who do not intentionally seek out the truth, and even prominent feminists of colour have not always understood the question of Palestine as a decolonial question.[4]

The historic exclusion of Palestine from an otherwise progressive agenda has given rise to a well-known acronym, the PEP syndrome: Progressive Except for Palestine. And sadly, PEP is not today, nor was it ever, an exclusively white disease. Thus, while Palestinians and their allies welcome the NWSA vote as a significant and long-overdue recognition that justice for Palestine is a feminist issue, many disagree that it is a result of "the browning of the organization" rather than an overdue weakening of PEP among Black, Indigenous, Latinx, as well as white communities. And it would be naive, if not outright foolish, to assume some unfettered organic alliance among brown people around the issue of Palestine, or indeed around any issue of racism. This is because the nature of racism is such that it separates us, pits us against each other. Sadly, many Palestinians, as well as millions of other Arabs, have also absorbed the negative stereotypes about communities of colour that are pervasive in the dominant discourse and often can be and are racist against First Peoples, Black people, and Latinx. Additionally, the "oppression Olympics," or the competition to prove one's community or social group is the most oppressed, has proven detrimental to what, from the start, should have been a joint struggle against an overarching structural system of oppression.

My essay, then, will start with an overview of the challenges diaspora Palestinian activists, and our allies, have faced as we engaged with other feminists and "progressives" in the Global North—groups and individuals who we thought would have appreciated the intersections with our circumstances but who nevertheless failed to recognize the plight of the Palestinians as a gross injustice and a violation of a people's human rights. It then traces the advances we have made, among Global North and women-of-colour feminisms, as activists and organizers finally grasp that the struggle for Palestinian self-determination is a struggle for Indigenous rights and that feminist praxis entails engaging in solidarity with decolonial struggle. Finally, it ends with a call for Palestinians to continue the alliances we have forged or reinforced in recent years so that we can in turn contribute to the struggles of other criminalized communities, once (not if) we achieve our goal of self-determination and Indigenous sovereignty.

Liberal Feminism and/as Zionism

When, on November 25, 2015, the NWSA became the first gender focused, mainstream academic association to vote, by a significant majority, to endorse BDS, it seemed Global North feminism had come a long way from the days when a rude, clueless, and patronizing Betty Friedan attempted to silence Nawal al-Saadawi at the Conference on Women.

But this interaction between Friedan and al-Saadawi revealed more than the ignorance of one particular Western feminist about one of the pre-eminent Arab feminists of the time. It was, and in many ways remains, a telling illustration of the highly problematic Global North approach to Global South feminism. It is an approach that seeks, often actively, to decontextualize the circumstances of Global South communities and analyze them at the microlevel only, as if they functioned in a space of their own, immune to the macroenvironment of global politics in the form of colonialism, occupation, militarism, multinational labour, international trade, "development plans," or other such manifestations of foreign intervention. It is also an approach that continues to privilege Global North women over women from the Global South. For, as al-Saadawi pointed out, Friedan and other Western feminists at this same conference felt free to "bring up" politics in their own talks and analysis as they discussed solidarity with Black South Africans and ways to end South African apartheid. In other words, white women could discuss political matters, including the politics of other countries, but women from Global South countries were not allowed to analyze global phenomena and had to limit themselves instead to a denunciation of patriarchy within their communities. Global North women would then extend a helping hand in solidarity, to "save" their less-fortunate "sisters."

Such "global sisterhood," to borrow from the title of an anthology edited by one of Friedan's peers, Robin Morgan, does not allow for being on an equal footing, and it certainly would not accommodate agency by the Global South women. The Sisterhood Is Global Institute, founded by Morgan and Simone de Beauvoir in 1984, has not endorsed the Palestinian call for BDS and has not replied to my requests for any comment about the NWSA vote.[5] This despite the fact that the majority of Palestinian women's and feminist groups, including the General Union of Palestinian Women and Palestinian Federation of Women's Action Committees, are among the initiators and signatories of the 2005 call for BDS, a call for solidarity with the Palestinian people modelled upon the call for solidarity with Black South Africans US feminists had embraced in the 1980s. This nonviolent campaign calls for broad boycotts and divestment initiatives against Israel until it meets its obligations under international law:

1. Ending its occupation and colonization of all Arab lands and dismantling the wall.
2. Recognizing the fundamental rights of the Arab-Palestinian citizens of Israel to full equality.
3. Respecting, protecting, and promoting the rights of Palestinian refugees to return to their homes and properties as stipulated in UN Resolution 194.

There is actually nothing "radical" in these goals, as they are based in the context of human rights and merely demand of Israel that it stop violating international law. Thus the refusal to address Palestinian women's issues as feminist issues, and the dismissal of Palestinian women's repeated calls for solidarity against a brutal occupier, are indications that Global North feminism is still ill-equipped to deal with a women's agenda that denounces colonialism rather than whatever version of homegrown patriarchy happens to impact us. Yet feminism, according to Palestinian scholar Nadera Shalhoub-Kevorkian, "entails understanding the nature and significance of solidarity with the dispossessed, something that global feminism, international law, and Israeli feminism have so far failed to do" as far as Palestinian women are concerned.[6]

More importantly for our present discussion, the

Global North feminist approach has long singled out Israel for immunity from any criticism while also seeking to censor any discussion of that country's oppressive policies. Global North feminists, like so many Global North liberals, do not want to "bring up politics," especially where Israel is involved. Yet they have no such inhibitions when it comes to criticizing other overtly political aspects of sexism and gender inequity. It is certainly ironic that the activists who argued that "the personal is political," a mantra of 1960s white feminism (or "second-wave feminism," as it is generally known in the dominant discourse) would deny that the political has a personal impact—especially on Global South women who fall at the intersection of various overarching oppressive structures. Nevertheless, this "hegemonic feminism" is the one that characterized mainstream discourse until recently, despite the simultaneous (not latecomer) existence of a more radical, more comprehensive analysis by women of colour. If Sojourner Truth's "Ain't I a Woman" speech remains insufficient proof that women of colour have always been alienated from hegemonic feminism and have questioned it from the very start, rather than at a later stage, then Becky Thompson's (2002) excellent "Multiracial Feminism, Recasting the Chronology of Second Wave Feminism" provides rigorous evidence.[7] Nevertheless, even within women-of-colour feminism, some have simply never considered the plight of the Palestinians as a critical decolonial feminist issue, while others yet hold on to the mainstream belief that Palestinians, not Israelis, are at fault in occupied Palestine.

The phenomenon of shielding Israel from criticism

has plagued the West for decades. As a result, it has blinded a majority of Global North activists to the fact that the greater oppressor of Palestinian women is not Islamic fundamentalism but Zionism, which has rendered the entire Palestinian people a dispossessed, disenfranchised people whose very human rights Israel violates daily. Thus we continue to see antiwar activists denouncing the US occupation of Iraq but not Israel's occupation of Palestine, as if unaware of the parallels between the two. For example, in 2012, at a progressive African American event in Seattle, where I was gathering signatures for a petition to have the City of Seattle divest from companies that benefit from Israel's illegal occupation, a white, self-identified Jewish American woman attempted to talk me out of my endeavour, patronizingly telling me I was "naive" to seek to connect oppressions and surely would not do so if I understood what was going on in Israel. When I explained that, as a seasoned Palestinian activist with first-hand knowledge of the situation, I would not describe myself as "naive," she switched to calling me antisemitic and sought to have me ousted from the event.

While quick to denounce the oppression of Arab women as a result of Islamic fundamentalism but not as a result of Israeli occupation, Western feminists seem oblivious to the fact that the gendered manifestations of occupation and militarism aggravate women's circumstances in Palestine, as they would anywhere else. These feminist scholars are eager to analyze the feminization of poverty in other war-ravaged countries, but when it comes to Israel many Western feminists' critical analysis fails to grasp the gendered aspects of Israel's oppression of the Palestinian people. The myopic lens looks only at the microenvironment, namely Arab society, and completely overlooks the macroenvironment, namely Israel's occupation, its harsh discriminatory measures, and its violation of the Palestinian people's human rights.

When the circumstances of Palestinian women are considered at all, it is generally a denunciation of "life under Hamas rule." Yet Palestinian women have been explaining for decades that they are at least as much, if not more, oppressed by Israel and Zionism than they are by their fellow Palestinian men. As Camille Odeh told Nadine Naber, the United Palestinian Women's Association was holding workshops on Palestine as part of radical anticolonial organizing as early as the 1980s.[8] Many Arab diaspora feminists have written essays explaining that solidarity with Palestinian women entailed denouncing and organizing to end Zionism as a settler-colonial project. In my own essay, "The Burden of Representation," I explain that Palestinian women's freedom of movement, their right to an education, their right to vote, to work, to live where they want, where they were born, their right to sufficient food, clean water, and medical treatment in their own homeland are denied them not by their fellow Palestinians but by the illegal occupying power, Israel.[9] This most basic reality seems too challenging for disingenuous liberals, who prefer to focus on dress codes and the outwardly trappings of "emancipation" and persist in silencing criticism of Israel with retorts about "Islamic" patriarchy or fundamentalism. Haneen Maikey, director of the queer Palestinian group AlQaws, recently captured the frustration of many Palestinian feminists when she commented, in a Facebook post:

> In today's meeting [with representatives of international organizations] one popular question was raised again by a staff who lives and works in Jerusalem for few years now: "how alQaws operates in Jerusalem, a very conservative place?" In an attempt to stay polite I replied with "why conservative would be the main framework of talking about Jerusalem or gay people in Palestine?" Why not occupied; economically marginalized; a place that it's crucial social and political characterization is being changed and shaped by new settlements, and systematic house demolishing; or by the fact your right to live in your hometown is threatened on a daily base; a society that it's young generation is being executed on its streets; why not colonized, statelessness, poor, and, yes, also "conservative"?[10]

The attempts to frame sexuality through the lens of norms and tradition is not only racist and convenient but also far from capturing the endless forms of violence practised on LGBT communities in Palestine.

On the theoretical level, it is generally accepted that hypermilitarism, occupation, and settler colonialism are inevitably accompanied by gender violence. The very language we use to refer to acts of land appropriation is reflective of this violent coupling. An expression such as "penetration into virgin land," which was quite common

in the days of European conquest of the African continent, or "the rape of Gaza," which we hear again and
again with every Israeli assault on the besieged region,
are historical and daily reminders of this mentality. The
men whose land is conquered are considered "emascu-
lated," their failure to protect the land apparently reveals
them as "effeminate." This is all highly sexualized language of domination and violence. Of course, we are
also sadly familiar with the expression "rape, pillage,
burn," which accompanies conquest, and we know
that women are "the spoils of war." Wherever we look,
gendered violence is an integral part of conquest and of
settler colonialism. Israel, a brutal military occupying
power constantly expanding its illegal settlements, is no
exception. Specifically, when such a power views a population—its dispossessed, disenfranchised, and occupied
Indigenous population—as a "demographic threat," that
view is fundamentally both racist and gendered.

And racist population control relies specifically
on violence against women. So it is not surprising that
Mordechai Kedar, an Israeli military intelligence officer
turned academic, would matter-of-factly suggest that
"raping wives and mothers of Palestinian combatants"
would deter attacks by Hamas militants.[11] Similarly,
Israeli lawmaker Ayelet Shaked did not attempt to present
the murder of Palestinian children and their mothers as
unfortunate, disproportionate collateral damage; she
openly called for it by asserting that Palestinian women
must be killed too, because they give birth to "little
snakes."[12] Yet Palestinian mothers, like mothers everywhere, have one overwhelming concern: sheltering their

children from harm. In Palestine, that harm comes from the Israeli military and the Israeli settlers. Many mothers comment on the fact that it is impossible to avoid being politicized at an early age, as children cannot be sheltered from the Israeli violence all around them. Others actually want their children to understand the gravity of the situation, so as to better confront it. Yet others, like Fatmeh Breijeh, for example, encourage resistance for liberation. Breijeh, of Al Ma'sara, near Bethlehem, explains:

> I have decided to continue to resist until the last breath and to continue to urge people to resist and to teach my children to resist and to lay the foundation for this through their milk. Our roots are fixed here. We, this land, this land, we are from this land. Look at the earth, at the soil; you will find it's our color. Every blade of grass, we know. They don't know anything. They only know to carry weapons and to steal—to steal the water, to steal the blessings of our land—everywhere.[13]

The resistance Breijeh has decided to teach her children is, above all, a resistance that consists of an Indigenous woman's defiant persistence, a rooted resistance that stems from knowing every blade of grass, rather than the behaviour of Israeli soldiers and settlers who "only know to carry weapons and to steal."[14]

"Sisterhood Is . . ." Selective?

The differing views in the Global North about Palestine have tended to fall, broadly speaking, along race and its attendant socioeconomic lines. However, many disenfranchised, progressive women of colour in the Global North had also absorbed the hegemonic discourse, with the Zionist narrative underlying it, and also failed for a long time to view the question of Palestine in a colonial context. As Simona Sharoni and Rabab Abdulhadi write in their essay published shortly before the historic 2015 NWSA vote, and a full thirty years after the Saadawi-Friedan encounter:

> For years, feminists in the Global North have failed to understand why Palestinian women insist on linking their struggles for gender equality to national liberation. As a result, Palestinian women have been at the receiving end of well-intentioned but misguided initiatives, which have disregarded their agency, needs and resilience, and have focused on a narrow understanding of "women's issues" and critiques of patriarchy and nationalism . . . Missing from the feminist response to the crisis in Palestine has been recognition of its root causes, namely Israel's illegal occupation of the West Bank and Gaza Strip, its violation of Palestinian rights and its apartheid-like policies toward the Palestinian people."[15]

Indeed, for many decades, hegemonic feminism in the Global North was dominated by middle-class women of European descent grappling with the unmitigated trauma of the Holocaust. These include Betty Friedan, author of one of the more influential feminist manifestos of the twentieth century, *The Feminine Mystique*, who had tried to censor Nawal al-Saadawi at the International Conference on Women; Robin Morgan, author of the book *Sisterhood is Powerful*, and cofounder of the Sisterhood Is Global Institute; Gloria Steinem, founder of *Ms. Magazine*; Shulamit Firestone, radical feminist author of *The Dialectic of Sex*; and other such towering women who were either raised Jewish in the immediate aftermath of the Holocaust or educated to denounce antisemitism, and a few other forms of racism, as the ultimate evil. To these white women, the European discourse, and European suffering, is in a class apart, and above, any other suffering. Thus, in hegemonic discourse, there is still no acknowledgement, to this day, that European imperialism led to the violent deaths of tens of millions of Africans on the continent itself, in addition to the millions who were enslaved in Europe and the Americas.

Nobel laureate Toni Morrison tried to inscribe the magnitude of this horrific episode in the US national consciousness when she dedicated her best-selling novel *Beloved* to the "sixty million and more" enslaved Africans who perished in the slave trade, but the reminder was pushed aside in the all-American focus on the individual rather than the collective. And despite widely documented atrocities committed by King Leopold II in the Congo, the Belgian monarch is never named as a murderous historical leader in line with non-Westerners such as Pol Pot, Idi Amin, or Genghis Khan. Consequently, despite the devastation wreaked by Europeans on the rest of the world throughout modern history, the only European who is unanimously acknowledged as evil is Adolf Hitler, whose victims were primarily Europeans. In other words, when Europeans ravage non-European countries, their crimes are not viewed as such, but are misrepresented and generally sanitized instead as "discoveries" (as in the case of the Spanish conquest of the Americas), "mandates" (as in the case of Britain's cavalier deciding of the fate of Palestine), or "civilizing missions," as in France's devastating colonization of Algeria, Morocco, and Tunisia. The US has even coined what must be one of the greatest euphemisms of all times, describing its brutal enslavement of millions of Africans and their descendants as "the peculiar institution." In North America, in what is today the United States of America, 90 percent of the Indigenous peoples were killed within 150 years of the arrival of Christopher Columbus. Yet he is celebrated as a discoverer rather than a murdering conqueror. Somehow, genocides of the magnitude of what Columbus launched against the Indigenous peoples of North America, or what the European slave trade did to Africans, do not register like that of Europe's Jewish communities because the victims were not European. Indeed, the frequent statement that six million Jews perished in the Holocaust, or more correctly the omission of the fact that an almost equal number of other communities also perished in the Holocaust because of whatever accident of birth made them "other," is proof that Jewish suffering is elevated above the suffering of others: the Roma, twins, gays and lesbians, as well as Africans. Yet Hitler was also intent on "cleansing" Europe of those "undesirables," who are so often forgotten.

In such a whitewashed context, it is surprising, to say the least, to read Gloria Steinem stating that her own feminism had always been indebted to Black feminism. "I learned feminism disproportionately from black women," Steinem said in a December 2015 interview, adding that, in her view, feminism had always been intersectional because it had always been aware of class and race.[16] She went so far as to say that Black women "invented feminism."[17] But even if one were to grant that Steinem's feminism had indeed been aware of both class and race, merely acknowledging a white debt to Black contributions in the US does not translate into a critical understanding of structural oppressions as lived by people of colour. All too often, it is no more than bad-faith lip service to "diversity," an attempt to alleviate white guilt by professing that one has been "influenced by," rather than exploitative of, the experiences of people of colour. This is most obvious in the music industry, which acknowledges the seminal contributions of African Americans to rock and roll, jazz, hip hop, rap, yet continues to disproportionately reward white artists exploiting these Black genres over African Americans performing them.

Breaking Through the Censorship: Zionism Is Racism

Growing up in the Global North, women of colour who did not intentionally seek out political analysis from the Global South around the question of Palestine assimilated the white, mainstream presentation of the resistance of the Palestinian people as another episode of violent anti-semitism, continuing the age-old (if European) hounding of the Jewish people. The hegemony of white feminism began to crumble and fritter away in the 1980s and 1990s with the publication and overwhelmingly positive reception of groundbreaking anthologies like *This Bridge Called My Back*, *Hacienda Cara*, and *Third World Women and the Politics of Feminism*.[18] At long last, a more nuanced analysis began to gel and to infiltrate most feminist communities. Young women now still read Steinem and de Beauvoir, as if de rigueur, but also became familiar with bell hooks and Audre Lorde. Introduction to women's studies courses, which had once been as exclusively white and exclusively about men's conflicts and territorial battles as history textbooks, began to incorporate one or two essays by women of colour. But these essays frequently remained "oppositional," even optional, denouncing and thus simultaneously reinforcing the white metanarrative. Concepts such as double jeopardy and multiple jeopardy, while dealing a blow to the sense of victimhood of middle-class white women suffering from ennui in the luxury of their comfortable homes, were still viewed as the plight of "minorities" rather than that of the majority of people everywhere.

And many women of colour still held on to the hegemonic representation of Palestine, despite an otherwise critical analysis of colonialism. Specifically, many women of colour, including Indigenous women, held on to the mainstream vilification of the Palestinians, now viewed as the age-old enemy of the Jewish people rather than the recent victims of Zionism. With the global "War on Terror," the Orientalist fascination with veiled women, the odalisque, the harem, gave way to an unbridled Islamophobia that viewed all Palestinians, women, men, and children, as would-be murderous terrorists harbouring evil intentions of "throwing the Jewish people into the sea." The supposedly feminist Israeli prime minister Golda Meir is reputed to have declared, "Peace will come when the Arabs [Palestinians] love their children more than they hate us." While the accusation cannot be directly sourced, its wide currency in Zionist circles is a clear indication of a mindset that blames Palestinians, a colonized dispossessed people, for "hating Jews" rather than seeking to overthrow their occupier.

The transposition of centuries of European antisemitism onto the Palestinian people, even though Palestinians had historically been a genuinely diverse community, both racially and religiously, remains one of the successes of the Zionist narrative of victimhood. Today, we hear that "Muslims and Jews have been fighting for centuries," a statement that simply cannot be corroborated despite an extremely well-documented history of the region, or that "the Palestine-Israel conflict is an ancient one," an ahistorical statement if ever there was one, as Israel was only created in 1948, with Palestinians resisting their dispossession since they learned about the plans to carry it out. And despite the (erroneous) claims that "the people in that region have always been fighting each other," the accusing finger in such statements is always pointed at the non-Jewish communities to perpetuate the victimhood and historical suffering of the Jews. There is no acknowledgement that, as far as diverse communities go, the people of Palestine are actually exceptional in how little internecine fighting they engaged in, until Zionism rent them asunder and privileged some of them (the Palestinian Jewish community, and later, other Arab Jews) over the rest of the Indigenous people. Regional and European Jews, then, non-native to Palestine, became Palestine's new coloniz-ers, and Palestinian resistance was not predicated on their religion but rather on the fact that the Palestinian people were being dispossessed, displaced, disenfranchised, and denied their most basic human rights by a newly settled immigrant community, with special rights and privileges only they could enjoy. And Zionism was certainly not rec-ognized for the racist ideology that it was, and remains, in its determination to grant the settler-colonial members of one specific community privileges that the non-Jewish Indigenous people of the land, now rendered "outsiders," do not enjoy. Even among feminists-of- colour circles in the West, very few questioned that narrative. There were exceptions, of course, as stated above.[19] Yet, overall, the experience of many Arab American feminists denouncing Zionism was one of alienation, invisibility, and, fre-quently, outright hostility.[20]

In "The Forgotten '-ism,'" members of the San Francisco chapter of the Arab Women's Solidarity Association broke through decades of print censorship when they courageously named Zionism for what it is: an oppressive and violent system of racism that lashes out at anyone questioning its righteousness. The authors of this courageous essay wrote:

As Arab women activists, we had been calling for Palestinians' right to self-determination, resisting the censorship of Arab voices on multiple fronts: in the media, in public lectures, in our classrooms, in our workplaces, and among our friends and colleagues. Upon comparing notes and experiences, we found that each of us had been harassed, intimidated, and sabotaged by supporters of Zionism trying to silence our resistance. We realized that while we had been feeling alienated and unsupported in our daily claims for Arab human, social, political and national rights and human dignity, we were not alone—the voices of Arab American women activists are regularly policed and silenced.[21]

For, while the groundbreaking women-of-colour anthologies had opened the floodgates of intersectional feminist scholarship and analysis, Arab women remained censored because Zionism—meaning the evil they denounced above all else—was misrepresented, "whitewashed" by the mainstream, made to look—as so many crimes committed throughout history by Europeans are—as a "civilized" (if not quite civilizing) mission, beset by hostile attackers. "The Forgotten '-ism,'" with Nadine Naber, Eman Desouky, and Lina Baroudi as principal writers, was first published by the Women of Color Resource Center and reprinted in *The Color of Violence*, edited by the INCITE! Women of Color Against Violence collective. INCITE!, which did not necessarily start out with a solid understanding of the question of Palestine, nevertheless fully understood it when some members introduced it to the national steering collective and has centralized it in its analysis since the early 2000s. Indeed, INCITE! has made an endorsement of its Palestine Points of Unity a requirement for national chapters, has created popular education materials on Palestine, and has facilitated or sponsored workshops on Palestine for years now. One cannot overestimate the courage and integrity it took for the Arab diasporan activists to research and write "The Forgotten '-ism,'" or for the Women of Color Resource Center, and later INCITE!, to publish it. Even today, speaking out against Zionism requires courage that few have and comes with very harsh consequences, as evidenced by the vicious personal and professional attacks on organizers for Palestinian rights, the calls for firing faculty who are sympathetic to the Palestinian cause, the actual firing of some such faculty, and the fully justified fears of pro-Palestine students and teachers that they will not be hired. There are over thirty Zionist organizations in the US monitoring the syllabi, lectures, and publications of faculty who are supportive of Palestinian rights, and the recently formed Canary Mission focuses on student organizers and tries to influence potential employers not to hire them. As these McCarthyist organizations multiply, coalitions and legal defence teams are organizing to counter them. But almost three decades ago, it was best for most not to profess views that acknowledge the humanity and oppression of the Palestinian people. And very few who were not directly impacted by Zionism did.

In his documentary *Peace, Propaganda, and the Promised Land*, University of Massachusetts-Amherst communications and cultural studies professor Sut Jhally explained that for years, he regularly conducted surveys of his first-year students geared at revealing their general knowledge of international affairs.[22] These surveys showed that 75 percent of students believed the

Palestinians were occupying Israel, not the other way around. This statistic is significant in revealing the level of ignorance among otherwise privileged people and likely reflects the national unquestioning absorption of the Zionist lies. Palestinians and their allies were always put on the defensive, always presumed guilty, racist, antisemitic. Since we were overall viewed as the attackers, the invaders, the occupiers, our resistance was necessarily interpreted as terrorism, not decolonial struggle. Even today, the Zionist hold on the national discourse around the question of Palestine is such that progressives (not conservatives) celebrate condemnations of Israel's "disproportionate response" with little awareness that they are reinforcing the lie that Israel is merely "responding" to Palestinian provocation rather than initiating provocation because it is the occupier, the invader, the oppressor.

With the success of Zionism in dispossessing and vilifying the entire Palestinian people (men, women, and children, rather than a few hundred or thousand fighters), Arab and Muslim women no longer fit into the reductionist Orientalist lens that viewed them as oppressed by the Arab patriarchy. Besides, Palestinian women and their allies were actively rewriting that Orientalist narrative, explaining that they are more oppressed by Zionism than Islam. Rather than denounce conservative Arab society, these feminists were denouncing the harm that Zionism had inflicted on their communities. They were speaking out against colonialism and racism in ways that challenged white/Zionist hegemonic feminism, even as they remained invisible in women-of-colour circles. Jo Kadi, editor of *Food for Our Grandmothers*, the first anthology of Arab American and Arab Canadian feminists, spoke of Arab American feminists as "the most invisible of the invisible," while my own essay, "The White Sheep of the Family," published in *This Bridge We Call Home*, also decries our exclusion from women-of-colour feminism.[23] The extremely hostile environment that Arab American women encountered in the discussions among contributors to this anthology, prior to its publication, are revealing of how many so-called radical women of colour still spouted Zionist hatred of Palestinians and their allies, and sadly, the editors, Gloria Anzaldùa and AnaLouise Keating, sought to censor rather than support the latter, thus reinforcing the hegemonic, Zionist discourse.[24]

But there is a special kind of power in having nothing to lose. Stripped of homeland, freedom, dignity, and self-determination, Palestinian women continued to speak out. They wanted other feminists, activists, scholars, and organizers to see not only "beyond the veil" but also, more importantly, "beyond the *hasbara*" (Hebrew for propaganda). Along with the workshops and popular education we have been engaging in since the 1980s, some have organized and led delegations of Global North activists to Palestine so they would see for themselves the reality of Palestinian life under occupation, besieged and disenfranchised in our own homeland. The statements issued by members of these delegations upon their return to the Global North bear testament to the harshness of life under Zionism, as well as the determination of the Palestinian people to persevere, resist, and overthrow settler colonialism. Neferti Tadiar, for example, wrote that:

> To take a stand in solidarity with and to be involved in the struggle of Palestinians to resist and transform the conditions of their own dispossession and dis-posability—to join in their aspiration for collective freedom and self-determination—is also to participate in the remaking of global life, which cannot but be a paramount feminist act.[25]

Tadiar was part of a delegation organized by the US Campaign for the Academic and Cultural Boycott of Israel. Other women of colour joined another dele-gation, organized by Palestinian scholar-activist Rabab Abdulhadi, and they, too, upon returning to the US, issued eloquent statements of solidarity with the entire dispossessed Palestinian people. Change was finally afoot, and based on the multiple inroads we are making in various radical communities, it looks unstoppable.

Ending Zionism as Decolonial Praxis

Despite the occasional pain of betrayal by would-be allies, Palestinians are unwavering in their determin-ation to explain to the world that their desire for freedom does not stem from some irrational ancient indelible strain of antisemitism but rather from the very human impulse to be free, sovereign, and live a life of dignity. Palestinians know they have been dis-possessed by colonialism and that ours is a decolonial struggle. I argued in the opening of this article that the NWSA vote did not necessarily reflect a "browning of the organization," if only because such a statement would suggest that "brown feminists" have always been onboard the Palestine struggle for decolonization. Decades of activism in the US tell a different story, one of Palestinians and their allies struggling hard to chip away at the hegemonic Zionist narrative that depicted us, rather than our occupiers, as violent racist terrorists. This transformation happened first among feminists of colour, but it was certainly not spontaneous.

Nevertheless, despite the progress made in the Global North, a progress consisting mainly of the shattering of the Zionist narrative, Israel's racism is becoming more violent by the day (an average of three children were killed each day in October and November 2015). And each Israeli military assault on Palestinians not only takes the lives of hundreds of Palestinians but also causes miscarriages, pre-term labour, and stillbirths. Palestinian women in the Negev have the highest rates in the world of stillbirth, deaths during labour, and newborn fatalities. And these deaths are directly linked to Israeli restrictions on Palestinian movement and Israeli denial of access to health care to Palestinian women.

But it's not just Palestinian women and children. Even as we focus on women and children, we need to problematize the idea of "women and children" as worthy recipients of pity, sympathy, help, and solidarity as distinct from men, who do not deserve such help. As Maya Mikdashi points out in her aptly titled "Can Palestinian Men Be Victims?":

The killing of women and children is horrific—but in the reiteration of these disturbing facts there is something missing: the public mourning of Palestinian men killed by Israel's war machine. . . . We should be aware of how the trope of "womenandchildren" is circulating in relation to Gaza and to Palestine more broadly. This trope accomplishes many discursive feats, two of which are most prominent: The massifying of women and children into an undistinguishable group brought together by the "sameness" of gender and sex, and the reproduction of the male Palestinian body (and the male Arab body more generally) as always already dangerous. Thus the status of male Palestinians (a designation that includes boys aged fifteen and up, and sometimes boys as young as thirteen) as "civilians" is always circumspect.

In this framework, the killing of women and girls and pre-teen and underage boys is to be marked, but boys and men are presumed guilty of what they might do if allowed to live their lives.[26]

The denunciation of the killing of women and children, an expression introduced by Cynthia Enloe in the 1990s,[27] makes one ask if men can ever be victims. In my own research, I have also often commented on the fact that we keep hearing of a "disproportionate number of victims" being women and children, and so I ask, "What is a proportionate number of victims of any gender or age?" In reality, every Israeli policy, every Israeli assault, every massacre, can be named "Operation Kill Them All": men and women, children and the elderly, straight and LGBTGNC, Christian and Muslim. Feminism should not be so narrowly focused on one segment of the population that it ignores other oppressed communities. And all Palestinians are oppressed by Israel. This understanding is finally becoming central to the analysis of a growing number of intersectional, women-of-colour feminisms.

Justice is indivisible. As we look at our diaspora in North America, one mighty woman of colour looms large as one of the greatest heroes of this land: Harriet Tubman. Tubman was determined to free as many slaves as she could. She did not say, "If you are committed to nonviolence, come with me. If you have never committed a crime, come with me. If you believe in my God, come with me." She knew slavery was wrong, and she was going to free anyone she could who was enslaved. She knew that justice is indivisible, that freedom is a right for all.

Similarly, we need to understand that genuine solidarity with the Palestinian people cannot be selective when the entire people is dispossessed. Haneen Maikey, cofounder and executive director of the Palestinian gay group Alqaws, put it most succinctly when she told Western queer groups, "We don't want your solidarity if you only support us. You need to be in solidarity with all our people."[28]

Even as we focus on how Israel's policies impact Palestinian women, children, and queer people, we must keep in mind that intersectional feminism is not limited to improving the circumstances of some people. All Palestinians suffer from Israel's occupation, just as all Native Americans suffered from Europe's theft of this land, and just as all African Americans have suffered from enslavement and continue to suffer from institutional racism and structural violence.

Conclusion: Intersections, not Parallels

There are many long-standing alliances between Palestinians and various progressive women-of-colour feminists and radical anticolonial communities in the US generally. These may not have been highly visible until recently, when movements such as Black Lives Matter opted for a national disruption of (the) business of (death) as usual and insisted on publicizing the brutality of a murderous police force frequently trained in Israel. The shattering of the Zionist narrative that resulted from decades of Palestinian organizing in the Global North has also led to a greater understanding of the gendered aspects of settler colonialism in Palestine, leading many feminists in the Global North to a realization that the fight for Palestinian self-determination and Indigenous sovereignty is indeed a feminist issue. Along with the alliances that have sustained us, even housed us, for decades, we are now forging new ones. These alliances are long overdue and not to be taken for granted. They have required intentional work in getting to know each other's histories, in prioritizing strategies, in enacting and reciprocating solidarity when someone else's body was on the line, because of a deep understanding of intersectionality. Today, more than ever, there is growing consciousness that our struggles are not parallel—a term that suggests they will never meet—but intersectional, coming together at various nodes. Our hope is that the enactment of reciprocal solidarity is a long-term movement, not a "moment."

Today, Palestinians and other racialized, criminalized communities are coming together around imprisonment, law-enforcement violence, immigrant rights, border violence. We stand together in the struggle against gendered violence but also against militarism and settler colonialism. And it is incumbent on anticolonial activists and scholars to understand that the solidarity we are celebrating today is neither recent nor a moment. Instead, it is a long-standing movement, always in flux, ebbing and flowing as circumstances evolve and develop for our communities, but always there, always engaging with the greater oppressor, the system of racist colonial heteropatriarchy. With that understanding, and with the understanding that the system we are fighting is global, we can better appreciate that solidarity among disenfranchised, criminalized communities is not self-serving but mutually beneficial.

Globally, the connections we have made as BDS organizers are also very important and must not be abandoned once (not if) we achieve our goals. As the delegation of women of colour and Indigenous women wrote in their statement upon returning from their visit to Palestine:

> We were deeply impressed by people's insistence on the linkages between the movement for a free Palestine and struggles for justice throughout the world; as Martin Luther King, Jr. insisted throughout

his life, "Justice is indivisible. Injustice anywhere is a threat to justice everywhere."[29]

Speaking at the 1997 International Day of Solidarity with the Palestinian people, South African giant and Nobel laureate Nelson Mandela stated: "But we know too well our freedom is incomplete without the freedom of the Palestinians." Today, we can say in all confidence that "from Gaza to Ferguson" is more than an opportune statement, it's an understanding of long-term interconnectedness. And just as veterans of the South African anti-apartheid struggle are joining forces with us today, one day, Palestinians will say, "We know too well that our freedom is incomplete until all criminalized communities are free."

Decolonial Feminism and Palestine

An Interview with Nada Elia

By Liza Hammar and Francis Dupuis-Déri
Translation from French by Sarah Moses

First things first: Where is Nada Elia from?[1]

I was recently asked, at a conference, to summarize the "intellectual path" that led to my becoming a decolonial feminist. I replied that there had been no journey, no trajectory, I was simply "born against." I was born against organized religion, against hierarchies, against oppression in all its forms. So it is only natural that I would be a decolonial feminist.

My parents are from Jerusalem and became refugees during the ethnic cleansing that accompanied the foundation of Israel in 1948. I was born in Iraq, where my parents lived briefly, and I grew up in Lebanon. Today I am a United States citizen. But I was educated in Lebanon, in French, by Franciscan sisters. I remember stealing and breaking a small statue of Mary during the retreat before my first communion, in an early act of rebellion against religion. My father died when I was very young. At the height of the Lebanese uncivil war (which I will never call a "civil war"), my mother took us—my sisters and I—to England for reasons of safety.

When she decided to return to Beirut, I announced that I was going to stay in England, where I lived for a few years as a rebellious teenager, hitchhiking across the continent as I followed rock bands like Led Zeppelin, the Sex Pistols, and the Police. Curiously, their sexism wasn't enough to dissuade me from being a groupie. I was ultimately deported, under Margaret Thatcher, and had to return to Lebanon, where I went to university to finish my bachelor's and master's degrees, then worked as a journalist. After that I was offered a job at the American University of Beirut, which I liked enough to pursue my doctorate, so I could design my own courses. I came to the United States for that reason, and I'm still here. That's my personal "trajectory," in a few words.

What is your political and activist trajectory?

As I said, I don't recall a moment when I was not "against" oppression. So I never became a feminist; I was born a feminist, even if I didn't know the word. I grew up in a family of women, and my mother raised her four daughters alone in the diaspora. I was able to see the strength of women and understand our struggle, just as I saw that society preferred to depict us as weak and incapable of agency. I can't remember a moment when I was not conscious of injustice. I always reacted to it, even as a child. But being conscious is one thing and activism another. The latter arises when you understand that you cannot rely on others to find solutions. I grew up in Lebanon, where the politicians are a huge part of the problem and also benefit from the problem. Now, how could someone who benefits from the problem want and be able to solve that problem? And that's true everywhere! The solution must come from the people, the grassroots. So, at age fifteen, I started organizing in Lebanon. At the time, we crossed out our religious affiliation on our identity card—it's written in official documents. When those documents were confiscated, at one of the many checkpoints established during the uncivil war, we did the same thing with the new ones we were reissued. We knew that crossing out our religious affiliation was the solution, not the politicians' program to divide us in order to rule us better. Not long after, I became familiar with feminism as another form of resistance through social transformation. From then on, I've always organized within feminist groups: the Arab Women Solidarity Association,[2] the Radical Arab Women's Activist Network,[3] the Arab Movement of Women Arising for Justice,[4] INCITE! Feminists of Color Against Violence.[5] In fact, I was a member of only one group that wasn't specifically feminist, the US Campaign for the Academic and Cultural Boycott of Israel, where I was active for about ten years. Other than that I have steered clear of political organizations in the traditional sense of the term. I don't lobby politicians. That's not my approach because I don't expect politicians to be part of the solution.

What is the Palestinian Feminist Collective?

The Palestinian Feminist Collective is an organizing network primarily in the United States and Canada that arose from the Palestinian Youth Movement in 2021, in direct response to what some still call "honour killings," namely femicides—for example when a young girl is killed by her father for seeing a man she isn't married to (see "Multiple Jeopardy: Gender and Liberation in Palestine"). We noted the rise of an increasingly powerful patriarchal worldview in Palestine, of a regression rather than a progression, in large part the consequence of the Israeli occupation and hypermilitarism. We were inspired by the organization Tal'at ("stepping out"), which is made up of Palestinian women activists fighting this intensifying patriarchy. Their slogan is "No Free Homeland Without Free Women." Tal'at argues that for Palestinian women in the homeland, the problem is not only Palestinian patriarchy but also the Israeli occupation and Zionism. Our collective has adopted the same approach, and we take into account the liberation of queer people as well, as Tal'at has also been doing more recently. The most marginalized groups in any society must be free in order for that society to be free. Our objective is thus both national liberation and a social and political transformation. Otherwise, what's the point of it all? We've seen so many countries where women are still at a disadvantage—are at an even greater disadvantage—after national liberation. I've personally spent a lot of time studying the situation in post-apartheid South Africa, since we often refer to it as an example for Palestine, but it's unfortunately as much of an inspiration as it is a cautionary tale, an example not to imitate.

How can we envision the liberation of Palestine in the

future when the Israeli military offensive has continued for months and the accumulation of deaths and ruins in Gaza is unprecedented?

Personally, I consider Zionism to be bankrupt, collapsing, and believe we are currently witnessing its horrific agony, which is bringing down thousands of Palestinians with it. It is therefore time to consider what must happen moving forward and to lay the foundations for a just society: one free not only of Zionism but also of heteropatriarchy, of homophobia, and of transphobia. We must recognize that these oppressions are not simply the product of Zionist Israel; they existed in Palestinian society prior to it. With that said, Zionism has greatly exacerbated them. The objective of the Palestinian Feminist Collective is precisely to rid Palestinian society of all these problems, including Zionism.

In this context, how would you define feminism?

Feminism is a movement of love. I teach feminism and women's studies at the university level. Each term, I begin by asking the class for a definition of feminism, and I'm always surprised by their defensive suggestions: "Feminism isn't a hatred of men," "Feminism isn't radical," "Feminism is not separatist, nor does it seek to destroy society." I then ask my students: "Why are you trying to defend feminism as if it were a negative ideology? Feminism is positive and there is no need to defend it." The Palestinian Feminist Collective conceives of feminism as a positive force, a force of giving and social justice.

Our feminism has nothing to do with a hatred of men or the desire for a bigger piece of the pie. The imperialist and colonial feminism that I call "faux feminism" aspires for a bigger piece of the pie without considering how unhealthy that pie is. Let's take the example of Hillary Clinton or Kamala Harris, both of whom wanted to be president of the world's biggest empire, a hypermilitarized empire. That's not how I understand feminism; that's just false feminism. True feminism seeks to change the pie's recipe so it's completely different, which means an in-depth social and political transformation.

After the appearance of your article "Justice Is Indivisible: Palestine as a Feminist Issue" in 2017, have feminists in the United States been reacting differently to Israel, in particular after October 7, 2023?[6]

If we compare the current situation to that of five or seven years ago, I see support for Palestine growing and developing, even if there are still racist and colonialist feminists. There are still "faux feminists." The faux feminists are outraged and horrified at the rapes allegedly committed by Hamas militants during the October 7 attacks, and little else. As a feminist myself, I am completely opposed to all sexual violence and would never justify rape as part of the national struggle. However, the faux feminists are horrified by the violence allegedly committed by Palestinians but say nothing about all the sexual violence, which has been very well documented for decades,[7] committed by Israel against the women, children, and men of Palestine. And they say nothing about the ongoing genocide. Such an attitude is racist, brutal, and abject.

Why are the Hamas militants portrayed as "savages" when every day we see Israeli soldiers carrying out deadly destruction? Is this not "savagery," if one wants to use the word? We also see Israeli colonizers blocking the entrance of humanitarian aid—food and medicine—intended for Palestinian civil populations. Is this not "savagery" against a famished population?

At this stage, ignorance is no longer an excuse.

I've been teaching for almost thirty years, and over these years, teaching mostly young adults in their late teens to early twenties, I have found this age group to be increasingly conscious of Zionism being a racist and oppressive ideology, one that translates into violent settler colonialism on the ground. These young adults are also scandalized by what's happening in their country, the United States, which backs the genocide. They are well aware that Palestine is a feminist issue, a queer issue, an antiracist issue, and they want to know more about the subject. Today, we also see very diverse crowds at pro-Palestinian protests, including people of Indigenous, Latinx, Black, and Jewish descent.

What about the Jewish feminists in the Unites States you criticize in "Justice Is Indivisible"? In France, too, Jewish feminists such as Illana Weizman, who consider themselves to be intersectional, refuse to clearly condemn Zionism and claim their right to silence on the subject of the ongoing genocide. But in the United States, other Jewish feminists have openly taken a stance against Israel and Zionism. Judith Butler, for example, has publicly called for a ceasefire, the Palestinian population's right of return, and the dismantling of colonial structures. We think also of Rosalind Pollack Petchesky, who studied antifeminism and the new right in the 1980s. In 2021, along with Esther Farmer and Sarah Sills, she co-edited the work A Land With a People: Palestinians and Jews Confront Zionism, *and she was recently arrested twice in New York at age eighty-one while participating in rallies against the Israeli government organized by the group Jewish Voice for Peace. Does the Palestinian Feminist Collective have Jewish feminists as allies? Does it organize events with them?*

The feminists I criticize are Zionists, some of whom happen to be Jewish, and of course, there are Jewish feminists who are not Zionist, just as there are Zionists who are not Jewish. Zionism is a system of oppression; feminism is a force of liberation. It is therefore impossible to reconcile the two. Sheryl Sandberg, for example, is a Zionist who claims to be a feminist and has held senior managerial positions at social media companies. She recently wondered why there weren't more women and feminists siding with Israeli women denouncing the alleged sexual violence committed by Hamas militants.[8] Yet she has nothing to say about the hundreds of thousands of Palestinian women who have suffered Israeli violence for generations and are dying by the tens of thousands.

Fortunately, a large number of Jewish feminists are in fact our allies, including the leaders of Jewish Voice for Peace, as well as Sherry Wolf,[9] Alice Rothchild,[10] and Emmaia Gelman,[11] to name but a few I know personally. And our collective has a few members who are Arab Jews. Some of us organize regularly with Jewish Voice for Peace and the International Jewish Anti-Zionist Network, and we participate in panels together, sometimes coordinating group projects or events.

Surveys and studies conducted in Israel by Jewish feminists have also shown this hypermilitarized society to be marked by a high rate of male violence committed against women by partners and family members, among others, and against sexual and gender minorities. The situation is clearly not improving with the rise (and now consolidation) of the influence of conservative religious forces on Israeli political institutions. Though this is perhaps not the subject we want to discuss here.

On the contrary, the subject is not off topic, and we need to keep these questions in mind. It's very important precisely because Israel claims to be a progressive country that offers women and queer people optimal social conditions and political rights. There exists a whole propaganda apparatus to convince people of this, and false feminists and many queer people in the United States repeat it in unison, even though these groups are not safe in Israel, except perhaps in the bubble of Tel Aviv. Israeli feminists know there is a very high level of psychological, physical, and sexual violence against women in Israel.[12] The hypermilitarized politics have intensified the patriarchal tendencies in Palestine, but also in Israel, since militarism is a patriarchal, hierarchical, and violent phenomenon. When society as a whole is taught and trained in militarism, it is inevitably trained in violence and dehumanization, and its members are then more easily amenable to the idea of engaging in genocide. However, Israeli propaganda seeks to persuade the world that its society is forced to do what it does because of the Palestinians—that it is always acting in self-defence. One then forgets that Zionism is violent by nature, since it is a settler-colonial project, and that a land cannot be colonized without violence against the Indigenous people who live there. Colonization always requires violence against the Indigenous population. I repeat: Zionism is violent and there cannot be Zionism without violence. To claim that you have transformed the land, as Zionists do, is to admit that you have stolen it from the Indigenous to wipe out their presence.

There's the popular belief that Zionism was once an egalitarian socialist movement, gone awry. That's incredibly naive. Certainly, some early Zionists could have believed their movement would have no victims, but to still believe that today, you have to not see the victims. As soon as you open your eyes to this inevitable reality, you either remain a Zionist and accept your own deadly violence or you reject Zionism. There is no Zionism without victims; it's impossible.

What about the antiracist and decolonial feminists you also talk about in your 2017 article?

In that article, I refer to the anthology *This Bridge We*

Call Home.[13] Participating in the project was a very unpleasant experience, as we didn't expect so much hostility from our fellow contributors. It was proof of the horrible efficacy of Zionist propaganda and the pervasiveness of what I call "Zionism by default," which is widespread in the United States and best expressed in the unquestioned statement: "Israel has the right to defend itself." Hearing and repeating this statement ad nauseam, every time Israel launches an attack, leads one to believe that Israel is indeed defending itself, while what it's doing is oppressing others and defending its illegal occupation—and it has no right to "defend" an illegal occupation.

Unfortunately, feminists who think of themselves as radical, or decolonial, have been ensnared by the claim that "Israel has the right to defend itself," and "Israel is defending itself," without examining the political reality, which is in itself a symptom of Zionism.

But this incident dates back to fifteen years before I wrote the article that was published in 2017, and much has fortunately changed within feminist communities of colour today. Since then, we have redoubled our efforts to inform, explain, educate, and develop or reinforce networks of solidarity, to the extent that when a new crisis erupts, we don't have to explain everything all over again. It is perhaps unfair that we had to exert so much effort and energy, but the world is unfair and saturated with Zionist propaganda. I may come across as cynical, but I have to admit that Israel is currently participating in this collective education. Indeed, the televised massacre we're being shown—a genocide taking place before our eyes—is such that one has to admit we're right when we insist that Israel is an occupying force that violates international law and carries out mass killings.

What is the role of the diaspora in the Palestinian struggle?

In the US, we know we are participating in the colonial project, even if we didn't freely make the choice to be exiled from our homeland. As a settler here on Turtle Island, I do all I can to encourage the sovereignty of the First Nations. I consider myself an ally in Indigenous struggles here, and if the Indigenous people asked me to leave, I would. Moreover, I do want to return to Palestine, even if I'm prevented from doing so at the moment.

The Palestinian struggle is decolonial, since we want to return to tending the land that has been stolen from us. We also believe that the Indigenous people here should recover their sovereignty over their stolen land. But many of my Indigenous friends and allies have explained to me that they do not view Palestinians here as occupiers. Moreover, the understanding and solidarity between the Indigenous people on this continent and Palestinian women is getting stronger and stronger.

Aisha Mansour and Nadya Tannous, for example, are two Palestinian women activists at the Indigenous ecologist organization Honor the Earth,[14] while I personally have connections with the anticolonial and anticapitalist organization the Red Nation.[15] The First Nations recognize in us another Indigenous people dispossessed of their land.

To respond to your question more directly, the

diaspora has a large role to play in the struggle for the liberation of Palestine: we are in a privileged situation. For example, as I talk to you, I know I can take a break for a glass of cool, clean, and potable water. I have all the food I need. I have a roof over my head. I fear neither bombs nor snipers. It's an incredible luxury. On occasion, I'm asked: "How can you be so outspoken in your public talks, are you not afraid of retaliation?" I reply that I risk no more than the loss of my job, I don't really risk losing my life (yet, anyway). With this freedom and these privileges comes a responsibility to explain, to repeat, to speak loud and clear, and to relay the voices that come from Palestine but that are obscured by the sound of bombs. Since October 2023, the Palestinian Feminist Collective has occasionally led two, three, up to four popular education workshops on the subject a day! But it's not just "solidarity": despite the advantages of living in the United States, my rights too are violated, since I don't have the right to return to my homeland.

Fifty percent of the Palestinian people live outside Palestine. My mother, who was sixteen in 1948, is a Nakba refugee who fled to Lebanon, where she recently died. It breaks my heart that she, like millions of other refugees, could not go home.

How do you analyze, in the context of a critique of the State of Israel, the thorny issue of antisemitism?

It's exhausting to have to explain over and over and over and over again that antisemitism and anti-Zionism are two completely different things. Almost every time we organize events on campus, we feel the need for a panel on the distinction between antisemitism and anti-Zionism. These explanations drain our energy, and they're tedious, but we return to them repeatedly, and doing so is necessary precisely because the conflation of these terms is an intentional—and very effective—propagandist manoeuvre on the part of Zionists. As we explain, antisemitism is a form of racism, while anti-Zionism is an ideology or a political movement of liberation. I am absolutely anti-Zionist—I will never apologize for being anti-Zionist—but I am not antisemitic.

I don't deny the existence of antisemitism, I know full well it's widespread in the world, but Palestinian resistance is not a manifestation of antisemitism. We must remember that in the United States there is antisemitism on the part of white supremacists, for example, at the Unite the Right rally in Charlottesville, South Carolina,[16] where the crowd marched by torchlight chanting "The Jews will not replace us!" That is hatred for Jewish people. Antisemitism refers to hatred of certain individuals because they are Jewish. For our part, we don't hate Israelis because they're Jewish—we hate Israel because it oppresses us. It is completely logical for us to want to free ourselves of our oppressor. We demand an end of the genocide, an end of the violation of our rights; we demand freedom in our homeland. This is not antisemitism; it is the movement of an oppressed people whose land is occupied. It is anticolonialist, antiracist resistance. Indeed, we are seeing more and more Jews in the United States denouncing the genocide and Zionism, and it's not because of "self-hatred" or "internalized hatred." Clearly, if Israel claims to represent all Jewish people, it can also claim that our resistance constitutes antisemitism. This fallacious association is not happenstance; it is part of well-organized Zionist propaganda, which conflates all critiques of Israel with antisemitism, calls for a muzzling and censuring of such critiques, and places anti-Zionists on the defensive. In the United States, there is a campaign to have states and institutions, including universities, adopt the definition of antisemitism proposed by the International Holocaust Remembrance Alliance (IHRA). This definition provides eleven examples of antisemitism, seven of which are in fact critiques of Israel. The IHRA thereby maintains that it is antisemitic to claim that "the existence of the State of Israel is a racist endeavor," to compare "contemporary Israeli policy to that of the Nazis," and to ask of Israel that it respect the Palestinian people's rights because that would be applying "double standards by requiring of it a behaviour not expected or demanded of any other democratic nation."

If the State of Israel was as democratic and liberal as it likes to repeat, this type of critique would be protected by the right to freedom of expression. Israel would not claim it is hate speech needing to be condemned and prohibited.

One might want to condemn and prohibit antisemitic speech, but when I criticize Israel, as I frequently do, I risk being accused of antisemitism and being censured, under the pretext that anti-Zionism is a form of antisemitism. This is a weapon to silence critiques of Israel, pro-Palestinian voices, and Palestinian voices.

Further to this, what do you make of Islamophobia in connection with Palestine?

Islamophobia and anti-Arab racism are certainly at play here, but I think it's necessary to understand the particularity of anti-Palestinian racism. Palestinians are the Indigenous people, those native to the land Israel occupies, and while the majority of Palestinians are Muslim, there are also Christian Palestinians. Israel doesn't say to them, "Of course, as Christians, you're fine! We won't destroy your homes, we won't kill you, we'll respect your right of return." Similarly, Israel is on good political terms with several Arab states but refuses the idea of a Palestinian state. Even here, in the United States, many universities accept Arab, Muslim, and Jewish student associations but, especially since the Hamas offensive on the seventh of October, have prohibited pro-Palestinian associations such as Students for Justice for Palestine, and even Jewish Voice for Peace, since they are part of a pro-Palestinian network.[17]

In France, this distinction may be less important. The repression that has descended upon pro-Palestinian efforts since October 2023 is founded in the Islamophobic legislation of recent decades. And Hamas is associated with the Taliban in Afghanistan, the Islamic State in Iraq and Syria, and the Hezbollah in Lebanon, all enemies of the "war against terrorism," who represent the most retrograde forms of Islamic politics. In the context of the early twenty-first century, Hamas has thus been the perfect enemy.

Yes, and since Hamas is in fact an Islamic resistance movement, Islamophobia is very much at play in this context, when one associates all Palestinian resistance, and even the entirety of the Palestinian people, with Hamas.

One is reminded of the Palestine Liberation Organization (PLO) during Yasser Arafat's time, which organized plane hijackings and was called a terrorist organization. But we didn't speak then of religion or Islam. In fact, the PLO was socialist, which was far worse during the Cold War era.

That's one more reason to make the distinction between anti-Palestinian racism, which has its specific political manifestations, and Islamophobia. In France, Islamophobia dates back centuries, to the French colonial project, in particular in North Africa. The West has been Islamophobic for centuries and the United States has inherited this Islamophobia.

How is what's happening between Israel and Palestine connected to the United States, where you live?

I heard it said that before the creation of Israel, the United States didn't have enemies in the Arab world. I don't know who came up with this and I'm not sure I completely agree, but Israel is a hypermilitarized settler-colonial society, just like the United States, and depends on US patronage.

France is the second-largest arms dealer in the world. And these are also capitalist and imperialist countries.

Indeed, France and the United States are two capitalist, imperialist, and colonizer countries. Capitalism is immoral: what matters to capitalists is profit, not people. In any case, a significant part of the billions of dollars the United States allocates to Israel must be used to purchase arms from the United States. All of this is part of a military-industrial complex that feeds the war. Israel needs war, just as the United States does, because every oppressor relies on violence and war to maintain its oppression. Moreover, (former) president Joe Biden proudly repeated for decades that "if Israel didn't exist, it would have to be invented" and that the United States must not apologize for backing the Israeli state.

In "Multiple Jeopardy: Gender and Liberation in Palestine," you introduce the history of women who have been engaged, in their way, with Palestinian resistance since the 1920s. This reminded us of Patricia Hill Collins, who seeks to emphasize the importance of women—and mothers—in the African American movement via actions often considered "female," such as looking after children, establishing orphanages, communicating messages and information, taking care of the community, et cetera. At the start of the second chapter, which in particular looks at feminist networks in the United States connected to Palestine, you open with a quote by Nadine Naber, who refers to Wafa Idris, considered the first Palestinian woman suicide bomber. Then you don't discuss it further in the article. Why did you choose this reference?

I chose it because of the widespread admiration for Israeli female soldiers. Women serve in the Israeli army and this is glorified, and even considered a feminist accomplishment. Personally, I don't believe that when a woman joins the ranks of the army, it's in any way a gain for feminism. What's more, Israel is at war with the Indigenous people it colonizes and oppresses. I thus mentioned Wafa Idris to shed light on the discrepancies, the differences, between the glorification of women in the immoral, murderous Israeli army and the conflation of Palestinian women's struggle with terrorism. Yet, Wafa Idris is also a woman who chose to resist occupation. Why laud Israeli women who serve in an illegal, murderous occupation force but not Palestinian women who resist this occupation?

If we deplore Palestinian "terrorism," we should also, and especially, denounce Israeli state terrorism, which is much greater in scale and far more deadly.

Personally, I don't believe armed struggle is the solution—we will not attain liberation with armed struggle, even if it is our right to engage in such struggle. I return to the idea of feminism as a force of transformation, an ideology of love and care. We have to think about healing, about creativity, about the force of life. I believe in the right to resist, including with armed struggle, but just because I have a right doesn't mean I must exercise it. I have the right to do a lot of things that I don't do. But it's a right—I refuse to have it taken from me. Nobody is going to free Palestine with suicide bombings. We will free ourselves by creating different living conditions.

In fact, my next book consists of documenting and introducing the history of actions and initiatives carried out by women as part of the Palestinian resistance, including those women I call "protofeminists," who were part of the struggle before feminism was an organized movement. I approach Palestinian feminism from the perspective you just mentioned; that is, via acts said to be "feminine" that contribute to liberation: taking care of orphans, educating youth, feeding the community. This resistance began with the British Mandate imposed on Palestine and it hinges on the idea that we must also be free as individuals. As early as the 1920s, even before the creation of Israel, organizations of Palestinian women operated on two fronts: social and political liberation. When Tal'at says "No Free Homeland Without Free Women" it is just picking up a very old principle, one these women had already put into practice with their engagement more than a century ago.

This is obviously anticolonial and decolonial feminism. Everything these activists did was in the pursuit of national liberation: girls had to be educated for political liberation; the community had to be taken care of for political liberation; our culture had to be preserved for political liberation. And that required women's agency, women's empowerment. The chauvinistic approach often consists of repeating "National liberation! National liberation!" while that of women consists of saying "Women and queers must be free for complete liberation." Hence the idea that justice is indivisible. We can't bring justice to some people and not others. That's not justice—it's a privilege others don't have. Do we want privilege or justice? Justice is indivisible.

Notes

Chapter One

1. The phenomenon of holding on to "the old ways," frozen in a nostalgically romanticized past, is common to colonized societies around the globe and often manifests as a cementing of regressive practices.

2. Close to 80 percent of Palestinians are displaced, some "internally," only minutes from their historic homes, now occupied by Israeli settlers or left vacant, even as their Palestinian owners live as refugees, while millions of others are in the diaspora, scattered all across the globe, as Israel denies us the universally recognized human right of return.

3. Quoted in Nawal El Saadawi, "Forward: About Racial Discrimination Amongst Feminists," in *Color of Violence: The INCITE! Anthology*, ed. INCITE! Women of Color Against Violence (South End Press, 2006).

4. El Saadawi, "Forward."

5. At the time of this writing, the "Zioness Movement" and its parent organization, the openly aggressive Lawfare Project, have major disagreements over some of the positions the Zioness Movement has taken, and the fate of the Zionesses is uncertain, since their funding came from the Lawfare Project.

6. Israeli society is overall quite conservative, with some more tolerant or accepting "pockets," such as Tel Aviv. The Jerusalem Pride March, for example, an annual event started in 2002, generally meets with protests by conservative Jews—there were stabbings of marchers, by a conservative Jew, in both 2005 and 2015—and the 2006 World Pride march, scheduled

to take place in Jerusalem, was cancelled as a result of harsh objections by conservative Jewish communities.

7. For a more thorough discussion of pinkwashing, see Nada Elia, "Gay Rights with a Side of Apartheid," *Settler Colonial Studies* 2, no. 2 (2012): 49–68.

8. Tom Mcarthy, "Albright: 'Special Place in Hell' for Women Who Don't Support Clinton," *The Guardian*, February 6, 2016.

9. In a 1996 interview with Lesley Stahl, speaking of US sanctions against Iraq, Stahl asked Albright: "We have heard that a half million children have died. I mean, that's more children than died in Hiroshima. And—and you know, is the price worth it?" To which Albright replied: "I think this is a very hard choice, but the price—we think the price is worth it." "Democracy Now Confronts Madeline Albright on the Iraq Sanctions: Was it Worth the Price?," *Democracy Now*, July 30, 2004, democracynow.org.

10. The November 1917 Balfour Declaration is a public statement in which Britain's Lord Balfour informs Britain's Lord Rothchild of King George V's sympathy with Jewish Zionist aspirations. The entire statement, setting into motion European Jewish emigration to Palestine through a Western imperial cursory note that reduces the Palestinian people to "non-Jewish communities," reads: "His Majesty's government view with favour the establishment in Palestine of a national home for the Jewish people, and will use their best endeavours to facilitate the achievement of this object, it being clearly understood that nothing shall be done which may prejudice the civil and religious rights of existing non-Jewish communities in Palestine, or the rights and political status enjoyed by Jews in any other country."

11. Joost Hiltermann provides a good overview of Palestinian women's participation in the First Intifada in his article "The Women's Movement During the Uprising," *Journal for Palestine Studies* 20, no. 3 (1991): 48–58.

12. I have read, and heard, a few reports about this incident, some dating it to 1936, others to 1938. It is primarily recounted as oral history and does not appear in British or Israeli publications. A Wikipedia entry tells of the British military burning down the village of Baqa al-Gharbiya and taking the men away, in 1938, without mentioning the women's role in securing the men's release. While I do not personally question that the incident happened as oral history has preserved it, I would argue that, even if it were little more than a fanciful flight of imagination, the "story" is still revealing in that it shows women, not a few valiant men, as rescuing their kin.

13. Referring to the perpetrators of the Deir Yassin massacre as "Israeli" is anachronistic, as the massacre predates the creation of Israel. Specifically, this massacre was perpetrated by members of the Irgun and Lehi militias, which had been known to engage in terrorist acts.

14. I use "political" here in the mainstream sense of the word, even though I believe there is little distinction between the personal, the social, and the "political."

15. Palestinian women secretly sewed Palestinian flags, which were illegal, by cutting the right length of different coloured cloth in different homes so that if Israeli soldiers searched these homes they would find only red, or green, or black, or white cloth. Transporting the different components of the flag to one house, where it would be assembled, was a dangerous mission, which women undertook.

16. Julia Bacha, "Directors Statement," JustVision.org, 2017.

17. Bacha, "Directors Statement."

18. Bacha, "Directors Statement."

19. AlQaws "About Us," alQaws.org.

20. Abbas's four-year term as "president" (of a nonexisting country), whose powers are limited to subcontracting the Israeli occupation, ended in 2009, and he has stayed in office since, with no elections, through the support of Israel and the US.

21.   The details of the murder remain unclear, but the broad strokes are that this was a so-called honour crime committed by Israa's brothers and father. Israa's screams were recorded by an employee at the hospital where she was being treated for a spinal injury suffered during an earlier beating by her family members. Israa's very loud screaming, behind closed doors in her hospital room, was posted on social media and immediately went viral.

22.   Tal'at is a collective of Palestinian women formed in 2019. Their charter reads: "Women's emancipation must be prioritized and central to our liberation strategies, discourse, and action. We see that fighting violence and oppression of women and seeking justice and dignity for all must be recognised as the core of our National Liberation."

Chapter Two

1.   Quoted in Elizabeth Redden, "Another Association Backs Israel Boycott," *Inside Higher Ed.*, December 1, 2015, para. 7.

2.   I use "Global North feminists" here to refer to feminists geographically located in the Global North who have absorbed the Zionist narrative—a Global North narrative—whatever their ethnicity. Sadly, there are many women-of-colour feminists who fall within that category.

3.   Angela Davis, *Freedom Is a Constant Struggle: Ferguson, Palestine, and the Foundations of a Movement* (Haymarket Books, 2016), 34.

4.   I have documented some of our challenges within women-of-colour circles in "The Burden of Representation: When Palestinians Speak Out," in *Arab and Arab-American Feminisms: Gender, Violence, and Belonging*, ed. Rabab Abdulhadi, Evelyn Alsultany, and Nadine Naber (Syracuse University Press, 2011).

5.   I have contacted the Sisterhood Is Global Institute by message on their Facebook page, as well as directly through the

"contact us" button on their official website. My last attempt was in May 2016.

6. Nadera Shalhoub-Kevorkian, "Palestinian Feminist Critique and the Physics of Power: Feminists Between Thought and Practice," *Critical Legal Thinking* (2014): section 4, para. 2, criticallegalthinking.com.

7. Becky Thompson, "Multiracial Feminism, Recasting the Chronology of Second Wave Feminism," *Feminist Studies* 28 (2002): 337–60.

8. Camille Odeh told Nadine Naber (in press) Forthcoming in *Qualitative Research*.

9. Elia, "The Burden of Representation."

10. Haneen Maikey, "In today's meeting," Facebook, May 16, 2016, facebook.com.

11. Gianluca Mezzofiore, "Israeli Professor: Rape Hamas Militants' Mothers and Sisters to Deter Terrorist Attacks," *International Business Times*, August 1, 2014, para. 1, ibtimes.co.uk.

12. Ayelet Shaked quoted in Ali Abunimah, "Israeli Lawmaker's Call for Genocide of Palestinians Gets Thousands of Facebook Likes," *The Electronic Intifada*, May 8, 2015, translated post section, para. 5, electronicintifada.net.

13. Fatmeh Breijeh quoted in R. Najjar, "Life in Occupied Palestine Continues Quietly," *Biography* 37 (2014): 637.

14. Fatmeh Breijeh quoted in Najjar, "Life in Occupied Palestine."

15. Simona Sharoni, Rabab Abdulhadi, Nadja Al-Ali, Felicia Eaves, Ronit Lentin, and Dina Siddiqi, "Transnational Feminist Solidarity in Times of Crisis," *International Feminist Journal of Politics* 17 (2015): 654.

16. Steinem said this in a December 2015 interview, quoted in Stacey Tisdale, "Gloria Steinem on Black Women: 'They Invented the Feminist Movement,'" *Black Enterprise*, March 19, 2015, blackenterprise.com.

17. Quoted in Tisdale, "Gloria Steinem on Black Women," 1.

18. Cherríe Moraga and Gloria Anzaldúa, eds., *This Bridge Called*

My Back: Writings by Radical Women of Color, 2nd ed. (Kitchen Table / Women of Color Press, 1983); Gloria Anzaldúa, ed., *Making Face, Making Soul/Hacienda Caras, Creative and Critical Perspectives by Feminists of Color* (Aunt Lute Press, 1990); and Chandra Talpade Mohanty, Ann Russo, and Lourdes Torres, eds., *Third World Women and the Politics of Feminism* (Indiana University Press, 1991).

19.   For an in-depth analysis of the long-standing alliances between Arab diasporan feminists and the WRC in San Francisco, see Nadine Naber, *Arab America: Gender Politics and Activism* (New York University Press, 2012).

20.   I have documented instances of this hostility in "The Burden of Representation."

21.   Nadine Naber, Eman Desouky, and Lina Baroudi, "The Forgotten '-ism': An Arab American Women's Perspective on Zionism, Racism, and Sexism," in *Color of Violence: The INCITE! Anthology,* ed., INCITE! Women of Color Against Violence (South End Press, 2006), 97.

22.   Sut Jhally, dir., *Peace, Propaganda, and the Promised Land* (Media Education Foundation, 2004).

23.   Jo Kadi, ed., *Food for Our Grandmothers* (South End Press, 1999); and Nada Elia, "The White Sheep of the Family," in *This Bridge We Call Home: Radical Visions for Transformation,* ed. Gloria Anzaldúa and AnaLouise Keating (Routledge, 2002).

24.   I discuss this sad episode in "The Burden of Representation."

25.   Neferti Tadiar, "Why the Question of Palestine Is a Feminist Concern," *The Feminist Wire,* 2012, para 4, thefeministwire.com.

26.   Maya Mikdashi, "Can Palestinian Men Be Victims?," *Jadaliyya,* July 23, 2014, paras. 2–3, jadaliyya.com.

27.   See, for example, Cynthia Enloe, *Bananas, Beaches and Bases: Making Feminist Sense of International Politics* (Pandora Press, 1989); and Cynthia Enlow, *The Morning After: Sexual Politics at the End of the Cold War* (University of California Press, 1993).

28. Maikey, "In today's meeting."

29. B. Ransby, "Why We, as Women of Color, Join the Call for Divestment from Israel," *Colorlines*, 2011, para. 4, colorlines.com.

Chapter Three

1.   Interview conducted on March 30, 2024.

2.   International association founded in 1982 and chaired by the Egyptian feminist Nawal al-Saadawi, who worked to facilitate the participation of women in the political, social, economic, and cultural life of Muslim countries.

3.   This organization is no longer active.

4.   This organization is no longer active.

5.   Organization fighting violence against women and queer people, in particular sexist and racist police violence.

6.   Nada Elia, "Justice Is Indivisible: Palestine as a Feminist Issue," *Decolonization: Indigeneity, Education & Society* 6, no. 1 (2017): 45–63.

7.   For a general analysis, see Revital Madar, "Beyond Male Israeli Soldiers, Palestinian Women, Rape, and War," *Conflict and Society: Advances in Research* 9, no. 1 (2023): 72–88. For an analysis of sexual violence in Israeli prisons since October 7, 2023, see the report by Physicians for Human Rights Israel, "Sexual & Gender-Based Violence Committed by Israeli Military & Security Forces Against Palestinians in Israeli Prisons," March 7, 2024. In addition to the fifteen hundred complaints of harassment and sexual assault per year in the Israeli army itself, see Anna Ahronheim, "Out of 1,542 IDF Sexual Assault Complains, Just 31 Indictments Filed," *The Jerusalem Post*, January 5, 2022, jpost.com. See also Nada Elia, "Weaponizing Rape," *Jadaliyya*, January 19, 2024, jadaliyya.com.

8.   Sheryl Sandberg is also the author of *Lean In: Women, Work and the Will to Lead* (Alfred A. Knopf, 2023).

9.   An essayist and trade unionist, Sheryl Wolf is notably the author of *Sexuality and Socialism: History, Politics, and Theory of LGBT Liberation* (Haymarket Books, 2009).

10.   An obstetrician, essayist, and documentarist, Alice Rothchild is a member of the Jewish Voice for Peace Health Advisory Council.

11.   A professor of social sciences at Sarah Lawrence College, Emmaia Gelman is the founding director of the Institute for the Critical Study of Zionism.

12.   After the Hamas offensive on October 7, 2023, groups of women in Israel have sounded the alarm on the increase in calls for help by women targeted by male violence and on the possibility that men exercising coercive control over their spouses are among the tens of thousands of Israelis who have bought firearms, see Carrie Keller-Lynn, "Domestic Violence Exacerbated by Wartime, Raising Concerns over Looser Gun Policies," *The Times of Israel*, November 25, 2023, timesofisrael.com.

13.   Gloria Anzaldúa and AnaLouise Keating, ed., *This Bridge We Call Home: Radical Visions for Transformation* (Routledge, 2002), which includes eighty writings by feminists of different origins.

14.   For more information, see the "Palestine to Turtle Island" campaign, Honor the Earth, honorearth.org.

15.   Organization of resistance and struggle for the liberation of Indigenous people, from decolonial, anticapitalist, and ecologist perspectives, among others. See therednation.org.

16.   "Unite the Right" refers to a series of supremacist rallies that took place in the summer of 2017 in Charlottesville. Protestors opposed the removal of a statue of Robert Lee, a general in the Confederate army during the Civil War. Clashes broke out with counter-demonstrators. A twenty-one-year-old man rammed his car into the crowd at one of the counter-demonstrations, killing antiracist protestor Heather Danielle

Heyer and wounding nineteen other people. The murderer, who was sentenced to prison, is an admirer of Adolf Hitler and participated in Unite the Right protests with a shield bearing the logo of Vanguard America, a neo-Nazi organization.

17. In 2024, pro-Palestinian encampments had set up at tens of campuses in the United States, but numerous school administrations called the police to expel students and make hundreds of arrests.

Nada Elia is a diaspora Palestinian writer, grassroots organizer, and university professor. She is the author of *Greater Than the Sum of Our Parts: Feminism, Inter/Nationalism, and Palestine* and has contributed chapters to *Palestine: A Socialist Introduction* and *The Case for Sanctions on Israel*. She is currently completing *Falastiniyyat: A Century of Palestinian Feminisms*. She is a core member of the Palestinian Feminist Collective and has been the plenary presenter at major academic and activist conferences. Her articles have been published in *Mondoweiss*, *Middle East Eye*, and *Electronic Intifada*. Nada Elia lives in the United States, where she is an associate professor of Ethnic Studies at Western Washington University.